"If you are a new coach strugglin[...] a seasoned coach that has never bu[...] sustain your business, you need to buy this book and study it thoroughly."

— ROB ROELL, EXECUTIVE COACH,
EQUILIBRIUM COACHING

"Most coaches and business books only tell you what to do, but Client Attractor guides you through every step of the way. Jacob's process has helped me to integrate my unique authenticity to build an irresistible business offer, which has been critical to me in building a heart-centered business.

I highly recommend Client Attractor if you are looking to build a successful business that reflects your uniqueness and values!"

— PAM RAY, SPEAKER & CONSULTANT,
REALIGNING EDUCATION & WORKFORCE IN THE 21ST CENTURY

"A must-read for coaches who want to organically attract great clients using social media. Jacob's approach to client attraction is not gimmicky and adds dimension to the often-nebulous social media marketing and sales strategies.

It's a simple process that's easy to digest and implement, and it's helped me gain clarity about my ideal client and the confidence to authentically show up with purpose by adapting the process and scaling it according to my needs."

— ANITA R. HOLLINS, DACM, MSOM, MS

"Client Attractor *is the #1 book you need if you're an online entrepreneur, whether you're just starting out or wanting to get past a plateau. Jacob does a fantastic job of helping you understand how to create a rock-solid foundation for your marketing that will lead to easier sales. His methods are innovative and make sense...something that can't be said about a lot of the stuff from other so-called experts. If you want to have a successful biz, GET THIS BOOK NOW."*

— HEATHER SMITH,
ETHICAL BUSINESS COACH

"Client Attractor *has given us concrete tactics and systems that we have used to quadruple our business in six months. This process has helped us truly align with the natural flow and growth of our business. Previous coaches pushed us to only market high-ticket products without the foundation to really get there, but this teaches you how to get there. We cannot give this book enough stars!"*

— STEPHANIE & JENNIFER PAGEWISE,
RELATIONSHIP COACHES

CLIENT ATTRACTOR

ATTRACT HIGH-PAYING CLIENTS YOU LOVE, AND KEEP THEM COMING BACK

Jacob Ratliff

To request permissions, contact the publisher at info@jacobratliff.com.

ISBN: 979-8-9853348-0-7
ISBN: 979-8-9853348-2-1
First paperback edition January 2022.

Edited by Peg Robarchek
Cover art by Brandon Love
Layout by Julia Scott

jacobratliff.com

CONTENTS

FOREWORD

When I began coaching in 1997, there were only four coaching schools in the entire world. None of them knew how to market coaching services, much less teach their students to do so. When it came to marketing and sales, my only option was to throw a bunch of stuff at the wall and see what stuck. As a struggling coach trying to get started 25 years ago, I wish that I had someone like Jacob to provide the blueprint to guide me step-by-step through the process of finding clients.

In *Client Attractor*, Jacob has clearly captured the most fundamental and important aspects of what it takes to attract and land ideal clients. He takes the simplest and most elegant route to help coaches everywhere achieve the ultimate goal: an effortless stream of dream clients.

What's more, he does it with heart. I have rarely encountered someone who possesses not only the intellectual capacity to grasp what it means to be an entrepreneur, but also the compassion and understanding of the frailties of the entrepreneurial heart.

My hope is that you, reader, soak up the information in the following pages and use it to serve your highest good.

—MARY O'CONNOR, EPIC MIND CONSULTING

INTRODUCTION

WHEN I WAS FOUR YEARS OLD, I got the inspiration to start my first business. My parents and I, with my infant brother in tow, loaded into my mom's purple Toyota minivan and headed to Home Depot. It was a sunny spring day, and we were going to mulch the flowerbed that backed up to our garage.

The four of us walked up and down the aisles of Home Depot until we found the mulch. My dad found the exact type we needed— pretty enough not to be an eyesore, but effective enough to do whatever we needed mulch for in the first place.[1]

He pointed to the bag of mulch we needed, and his eyes dropped to the price sticker. "Gah," he said, "It's not cheap, is it?" He shook

---

1: I was four, I didn't actually know what mulch did besides go on the ground.

his head in defeat, and my parents set to work loading the bags onto the cart and then into the back of the minivan.

Back home, we set to work spreading the mulch in the flowerbed lining our garage. As we worked, I noticed that this mulch was just pieces of wood—pieces of wood that my dad had complained about being expensive only an hour earlier.

"Isn't this just wood?" I asked my dad, confused that he had just spent money on something we had so much of; after all, sticks and branches littered our yard from the thunderstorm we had just a few days before.

"Yeah," he said, chuckling. "Mulch is just bits of wood and leaves to help keep the soil healthy for the plants."

My mind started turning as I went back to arranging these wood chips around each plant. *Mulch is expensive, but it's just sticks and leaves. And we have both of those things.*

After lunch—a peanut butter and jelly sandwich on wheat bread—I asked my mom if I could pick up some sticks in the yard.

"Yes!" she said a little too enthusiastically. "You can get a trash bag out of the garage to put them in."

I went out to the garage and grabbed a single trash bag with my peanut-butter sticky hands—not one of those ugly black yard work bags that we always used when raking leaves, but one of the semi-clear ones where you could get a pretty good idea of what was in it if you looked closely enough.

While my parents returned to spreading their overpriced mulch across the flowerbeds, I marched to the biggest tree in the yard and started grabbing fistfuls of leaves, twigs, acorns, and anything else that would fit in my tiny hands.

Once the bag was half full, I tied it shut and started swinging it in circles above my head, watching the bag's shadow circle on the ground like a hand on a frantic clock. I kept spinning it above my head until I was too dizzy to keep going.

As I slowed to a halt, I stumbled towards that giant tree and clutched it for support, so I wouldn't fall to the ground. Once my head stopped spinning, I untied the plastic trash bag and peeked inside, pleased to see the materials all mixed.[2]

I scrounged up a cardboard box and Sharpie, and found my dad exactly where I left him, spreading mulch in the same flower bed by the garage. Once I got his attention, I asked if he would write something on the cardboard box that I had flattened.

"Yeah buddy," he said. "What do you want it to say?"

"Mulch For Sale."

"That it? Want to put a price on the sign?"

"Uhm, yeah," I said. "The price is free."

He wrote the price down and handed me my new sign.

"Thank you!" I yelled over my shoulder as I ran around the side of

---

2: Listen, no one had ever taught me about centrifugal motion and that it actually wasn't mixed at all.

the house to the front porch, my bag of mulch in one hand and cardboard sign in the other.

I sat down criss-cross applesauce on the big blue front porch, holding my sign up and waving at my neighbors as they drove past. All afternoon I sat out there, waving at every single car, until my mom called me in to eat. I set the bag carefully next to the front door—still as full as it was when I planted myself on the porch hours earlier—and ran inside for dinner.

"What have you been up to?" she asked as she scooped her famous (to me) chicken stir-fry onto a plate and handed it to me.

"I've been selling mulch!" I said with a wide smile, beaming up at her with pride. "I didn't sell any, but I'm going to work all day tomorrow and sell all of it!"

The next day, I didn't sell any—but not because I was discouraged that I hadn't sold any the day before. Rather, just because I was a four-year-old with a four-year-old's attention span.

But not to worry—my failure to monopolize the mulching industry did nothing to deter my entrepreneurial spirit; rather, it was the spark that continued to show up time and time again throughout my childhood and well into adulthood.

WHO THIS BOOK IS FOR

One of the biggest benefits of going full-time with my business was the time—the newfound time I had to take on more clients, and the time I had to improve my business skills and become even more of a master marketer and business expert.

I've always been an avid learner, so I was thrilled to jump back into learning mode. I decided that I was going to take every online course I could find and afford to hone those already sharp business skills even further.

Except it didn't work that way. I quickly realized that there was a gap: I was learning the *strategy* behind all of these business topics—digital advertising, content marketing, copywriting, email marketing, social media—but none of the actual *tactics* to make any of that work. It was like taking a CPR class where the teacher *told* you how to perform CPR but never actually *showed* you *how* it's done, much less let you try it on a CPR dummy.

I wanted to know why all of these courses were explaining the theory of these concepts but entirely ignoring what they actually looked like in practice, and it didn't take me long to find the answer. The courses themselves were just steps in some expert's sales funnel; the goal of the course wasn't actually teaching me, but rather priming me to buy whatever high-ticket offer came next.

But I wasn't yet in a place to invest thousands of dollars into working one-on-one with a coach, so I didn't. I just stayed where I was, all theory and no practical knowledge that I could implement.

I've heard hundreds of stories similar to this, and the truth is that there are a seemingly infinite number of resources and guides out there that talk about how to build your coaching business. The sheer volume of resources out there is overwhelming, and it's complicated by the fact that most of them aren't inherently wrong. They talk about creating and packaging your offer, generating leads, and making sales. It sounds a bit like this:

"You have to get in front of your ideal clients and provide value to them." Okay, but how?

"You need to position yourself as an authority." Makes sense. How?

"Provide value for your audience, and they'll want to work with you." Are you going to f—king tell me how?

All of these statements are true, but most of the books and courses out there entirely ignore what is arguably the most important piece of the puzzle:

How to actually do any of it.

It's perhaps the greatest blind spot of the whole demographic of coaches and businesses who supposedly help you grow your business—they can spout theory all day long, but when it comes to implementation they back into a corner and avoid the question at all costs.

Indeed, it's not limited to consumable resources like books and online courses. The issue of implementation avoidance also shows up when working directly with the self-proclaimed gurus who promise that if you shell out $10,000 to work with them, they'll help you make some ridiculous sum of money in the next three months.

The most consistent piece of feedback I've heard from my clients has also been the most surprising—that I'm the first coach they've worked with who actually took the time to walk them step-by-step through the implementation process.

My client Rob sums up this travesty 10x better than I ever could:

> *Jacob has an amazing ability to guide you through improving your process. I have run across a number of coaches who told me to do this, or do that, and very few of them spent the time to hold my hand through the entire process.*

I'm *tired* of seeing people shelling out money—for books, courses, and coaching—and not getting the actual support they need to create the coaching business they're dreaming of. That's why I'm writing this book—to show you the *concrete* things that will help you build a successful and fulfilling coaching practice.

Of course, this is still ultimately only a book, so there are limitations to the support I can provide you. The truth is that there is no one-size-fits-all strategy, which means that it's impossible for me to customize my advice for every single reader. What you'll read in this book is not a turnkey strategy that can be executed like Grandma's apple pie recipe, but rather a *concrete starting point* from which you'll experiment and tweak as you go.

My role is to give you the ingredients and the outline of a recipe. Yours is to take it and make it your own.

Sound daunting? I didn't promise that this would be easy. But I *can* promise that if you take the information in this book *and actually implement it*, that it'll be pretty damn simple.

Furthermore, this book is for coaches who want to make a difference—for coaches who know that they have something amazing to offer the world, and who want to change people's lives.

One of my biggest frustrations when I started coaching was that I *knew* that I had something valuable to offer, but I didn't know how to talk about it, much less how to get the right clients. Honestly? It was pretty disheartening, and I came to believe that nobody else thought my coaching was as valuable as I knew it was.

What I came to realize, though, was that it wasn't that nobody wanted to work with me—it was that nobody *knew* about me. Sure, they knew that I was a "coach," but they didn't know exactly who I was, exactly how I helped people, and exactly the transformation that I could help them achieve.

And those are just the people who were already in my network. Was I expanding my circle and connecting with new people? Absolutely not.

So, of course, nobody was working with me. *Nobody knew about me in the first place.*

This book is for high-impact coaches who find themselves in that situation—wanting to change lives but needing to attract clients whose lives they can change. This book is for coaches who are tired of getting sold into online courses, masterminds, and coaching programs that promise to help you attract new clients but that ultimately deliver no results.

This book is for the heart-centered, no bullshit coach who wants to attract their dream clients, and who wants to do it without slimy sales tactics.

Is that you? Then perfect.

Throughout this book, we're going to lay out the core components of an effective client attraction process. From here on out, we're assuming that you are a competent and committed coach (not necessarily certified), and that you have the coaching skills required to help your clients achieve real and sustained results.

In other words...we're assuming that you're a coach who's confident in your ability to serve your clients.

Because otherwise, this book is useless to you. Sure, you might be able to get some amount of success leveraging the strategies and tactics that I'm going to show you, but at the end of the day, what really matters is your ability to help your clients reach their goals.

THE FOUNDATIONS

THE HEALTH AND WELLNESS COMPANY I began my career working for had been around for 20 years by the time I came onboard, which meant that they had a long and impressive track record of getting results for their customers and clients. By the third month working for them, my boss was in love with me, impressed at the copy I was writing, the email sequences I was designing, and the new marketing campaigns I was proposing. She gave me a massive amount of agency to experiment with all kinds of different strategies and tactics, and somehow almost everything I did seemed to get results.

One of the most memorable projects I worked on was a four-day campaign focused on their online course. I was convinced the campaign would be a flop, but my boss pushed me to give it a shot anyway. The day the campaign launched, I nervously checked the sales numbers every 15 minutes, and each time I checked, the numbers kept rising. After the second day of the launch, I looked at the sales numbers again and couldn't believe my eyes. The campaign had brought in $20,000 over the past two days.

Some of the campaigns I worked on in that job performed better than others, but none of them was such a big flop that I was ashamed to show my face in the office. Did I have the golden marketing finger that turned everything I touched into new sales? Or was this just luck?

I started asking those questions even more fervently several years later when I left that position to start my own business. I knew the ins and outs of selling online, and I was chomping at the bit to get started. So, when I sat down to work on my business—to build the key elements that would bring me clients—I jumped straight to doing what I knew best: email sequences, lead magnets, Facebook ads, and website-building.

As I got into the weeds of building everything out, though, it started to feel a bit like pulling teeth. Everything I had to do felt ten times harder than it had been when I'd done it in the past for my previous employer. At my old job, I could churn out a lead magnet and email sequence in one or two days. But doing it for my own business felt impossible. When I *did* manage to finish something—to publish a lead magnet campaign or build out an email sequence—I only heard crickets in response.

Was it just luck, after all, or had my golden marketing finger simply faded?

The answer was neither; rather, something else was missing. The questions I had answered so instinctually at my old job were unusually difficult when it came to my own business; questions like what topic my lead magnet should be, how my landing page should be designed, and how my marketing emails should be phrased.

I was lost, but not because I didn't know how to do the things. In fact, the problem had nothing to do with my marketing skill set. It was simply because I didn't understand my ideal client and offer well enough to create a lead magnet, much less an entire email sequence. I had a vague idea that I was going to help entrepreneurs with their marketing, but that was pretty much as far as I had gotten. My understanding of my ideal client stopped at "entrepreneur" and "small business owner," and my understanding of my offering stopped at "marketing."

That's all I had to go off, so *of course I couldn't build out an effective marketing funnel.* Sure, I had built funnels like this in my previous job, but in that case, I was working from a rock-solid foundation that had been created well before they hired me. Their foundation was a crystal-clear understanding of their offer and ideal client, which had been established 20 years ago and had continually evolved ever since.

Years later, when I would finally create this foundation for my own business, it immediately felt as though I had switched gears on a bicycle to make pedaling infinitely easier. The resistance was gone. I was suddenly creating more effective content, having more (and better) conversations with prospective clients, and bringing on more clients than ever before. All because I had created that foundation.

Whether you're just starting your business or have been sharing your expertise for decades, if you don't have that solid foundation for your business, it's not going to succeed. Your business's foundation consists of these four things:

- Something to sell
- Someone to sell to
- A way to sell it
- A way to deliver it.

That's all there is to it. But the key is that while you need that solid foundation, *it also has to remain flexible*. One of the biggest benefits of growing a client-based business is that every experience you have is an opportunity to improve that foundation:

- Every strategy session or free consultation is an opportunity to get real-time feedback on your ideal clients' pain points.
- Every client you work with is yet another guinea pig for improving your process and practice (yes, *every* client, even if you've been coaching for a decade).
- Every social media post you make is an experiment in dialing in on your messaging, so you can speak *directly* to the types of clients you most want to work with.
- Every client you work with helps you better understand what types of clients you want more of—and what types you don't.

Before your foundation can evolve, though, you have to *have* a foundation. In this section, we're going to cover the four basic aspects of what will become your flexible foundation:

- **Your Ideal Client:** Getting clear on whom you serve, not just demographically, but psychographically as well.
- **Your Offer:** Creating a clearly defined offering that is built from the ground up for your ideal client, and that you can talk about in an easy-to-understand, sellable format.
- **Your Packaging:** Identifying the best way to fulfill your offer for your clients in a way that helps them achieve the best results.
- **Your Messaging:** Using language and crafting content that speaks directly to your ideal client.

In the next chapters, we're going to dive into each of these four aspects of your coaching business's foundation so that by the end of it you'll have a clear picture of whom you're going to serve, what you're going to help them achieve, and how you're going to talk about it to prospective clients.

YOUR IDEAL CLIENT

I mentioned that in the early stages of my business, I defined my ideal client as an entrepreneur or small business owner, and there are two reasons that I didn't get too far with that definition. The first might be pretty obvious—it was *much too broad*. "Entrepreneurs" alone is such an expansive category, encompassing everything from the successful drug dealer around the corner to the handyman I call when I need something done around the house.

As a result of not narrowly defining my ideal client, it was 10x harder to attract new clients because there was no way I could craft messaging that resonated with the massive demographic of people who identify themselves as entrepreneurs or small business owners (but more on messaging later). It also meant that I had a *massive* amount of competition—I was competing not only with everyone else who helps entrepreneurs and small business owners, but also with everyone who had a much more narrowly defined ideal client *within* that demographic. To say I was a little fish in a big ocean would be a massive understatement.

The second result of not understanding my ideal client was that I couldn't deliver a consistent client experience; I simply wasn't able to help them all at the same level. Like everyone else in the world, I'm better at some things than at others. But serving such a wide range of entrepreneurs and small business owners meant that I was doing some of the things that I'm best at, and much more of the things that I was fairly mediocre at. As a result, I was serving some clients much better than others, which meant that while a portion of my clients got excellent results, another portion of them didn't. Honestly? Not a sustainable business practice.

If you don't know exactly who you are selling to, you're not going to be able to communicate with them effectively—and that's why it's so important to have crystal clarity on who your ideal client is and where they're coming from. Therefore, the goal is to get so dialed into your ideal client that you can understand their perspective and create an offer that speaks to their deepest hopes and desires.

You've probably filled out a million ideal client worksheets by now—each one asking variations of the same questions: How old are they, do they have any kids, where do they live?

But those questions are *demographic-based*, meaning that their answers boil down to a specific tangible characteristic. These demographic questions are certainly useful, but there's a lot they don't tell us:

- What are their deepest desires?
- What keeps them up at night?
- What frustrates them?
- How are they spending their time?

The list goes on, but the point is simple: *Psychographic data*—information about the psychological trends of your ideal clients' mind—is a key part of understanding your target market. (Psychographics do not replace demographics, of course, but rather complement it.)

I'll share some of the questions I ask the most when helping clients dial in on their ideal client—and I encourage you to work through them. However, there are several important things to note as you reflect on each one:

- The questions themselves are fairly immaterial; the key is to use them as a jumping-off point for further exploration.
- The more specific and concrete you can get, the better. It can be easy to provide vague or abstract answers, but that will prove far less helpful when it comes time to put it to use.
- Remember that you're building a flexible foundation, so this won't be the last time you answer these questions. Make a routine of revisiting them every few months.
- Know that you might be wrong...and be okay with that possibility. It's fairly common to think that you know exactly who your ideal client is, but later discover that you were dead wrong.

YOUR IDEAL CLIENT IS A PERSON

The process of honing in on your ideal client is really the process of getting inside their head to better understand them. You're trying to really understand them, see the world through their eyes, and walk a mile in their shoes.

Throughout this process, the number one thing to remember is that your ideal client is an actual person. They are not just existing in the vacuum of what you can help them with. This is critical because you don't just want to speak to their concerns and their mistakes that they are making in terms of how you can help them—you want to talk to them in terms that encompass the entirety of their being.

For instance, if you're helping them with their business, their business is not the only aspect of their identity. If you are helping them with their health, their health is not the only aspect of their being, and the same with mindset, fitness. No matter what it is, these aren't the only things that they care about.

You want to get a more holistic view of your client. What else do they care about? What are their family concerns? What are their money concerns? What kind of communities are they in? Who are they talking to? What kind of friends do they have? What other relationships are they in?

We want to think of them as a whole person. If a person can be represented as a pie, each slice is one aspect of their identity. There are pieces for relationships, work, what they do in their leisure time, what keeps them up at night.

This helps you see the world through your client's eyes because this is how you're going to connect with them on a deeper level. It's not ever just about the thing that you can help them with because the thing that you can help them with, no matter what it is, inevitably spills over into other areas of their life. It has an impact on everything. And when you keep it at the surface, you really do yourself and your client a disservice because you cannot show them the impact of how you can help them as a whole person.

What causes them anxiety? What are they reading? What are they watching? What are they buying? What are the products, maybe other online courses, or people they are working with? What are they spending their money on?

You're a complex person, and your client is, too.

IDENTIFYING YOUR IDEAL CLIENT

Now, it's time to dig into the fun stuff—the questions to ask that will help you identify exactly who your ideal client is.

The first question to consider is *what is the result that you can help a business or a person achieve?* Your offer is how you help them get that result. But people don't buy the process by which they get to the result: They buy the result.

No matter who you are, there are probably countless different results you can help a business or a person achieve. However, you want to identify the most *specific* and *significant* goal that you can help them achieve.

Next, if you've worked with clients in the past, think back to them. Describe the best client you've ever had, and, more importantly, articulate what made them such a good client. Why were they your favorite?

The purpose of this is to construct a clear picture of your ideal client. Oftentimes, we as humans struggle when we're talking about abstract concepts. The same applies here—it's incredibly difficult to construct this image of an ideal client when you don't have a face to put on them. Therefore, when you can associate a specific person with your image of an ideal client, it suddenly becomes ten times clearer and more concrete.

If more than one person comes to mind as the image of your perfect client, even better. Instead of choosing one, simply jot down a list for each one, identifying the characteristics, behaviors, and situations that made each one so great. Then, take a closer look at those lists and see if you can identify the commonalities between them.

I once had a client who, when completing this exercise, couldn't seem to find any similarities between the people she identified as her favorite clients. On the surface, her three favorite past clients were an author, a coach, and an online course instructor—all in different industries and serving dramatically different niches.

As she began to get frustrated at not finding any commonalities between the three clients, we dug a little deeper and found that, in fact, they shared a similar mission and commitment that they brought to their work—specifically, they all were dedicated to creating positive social change. They just went about it in a variety of different ways. Once she was able to identify that common thread, she was able to name that as a key part of her ideal client's identity.

The next question to ask is *what's the single biggest problem your ideal client is facing?* If you're tuned into who your ideal client is, then the answer to this question should be related to the result you can help people achieve. It might not be a perfect match, but they should be very closely related.

What frustrates your ideal client more than anything else in the world? What gets under their skin? What really just drives them crazy? These things are going to end up being inspiration for content that you'll create down the road. The more work you put into this, the easier everything else is going to be.

What are the three to five steps that your ideal clients need to take for them to achieve this result? Your ideal clients need the result that you've already identified, so let's assume for a minute that you're talking with a client and giving them a series of simple steps to achieve that result. What are those steps? This is going to be the basis of your offer that we will explore when we talk about offer creation. For now, map out the concise, specific steps that your client would need to take.

What keeps your ideal client up at night? What are their deepest desires, anxieties, and frustrations? Remembering that your ideal client is a whole person and exists beyond the boundaries of the specific issue you help them with, don't limit yourself to things that are just related to your business and what you do and how you help them.

What specific event or occurrence do they desperately want to avoid that would leave them feeling humiliated? The difference between this and previous questions in the same vein is that here, you want to identify the specific events or instances that they want to avoid more than anything else; even more specifically, you want to identify the events that might leave them feeling humiliated or embarrassed. Avoiding humiliation is one of the biggest motivators for people. People believe they want to change or that they want to reach some specific goal, but oftentimes it's the avoidance of humiliation that actually spurs them into action.

For example, as a business coach who works with newer entrepreneurs, I know that my ideal client desperately wants to avoid a situation in which they start their business, eat through their savings, and ultimately admit defeat and get a job. It would mean admitting defeat to their friends and family. Because I know this is on my ideal client's mind, it becomes a very real concern that I can help prevent—which means that I can later build it into my messaging to motivate them to act.

At the beginning of this process, you identified the single biggest problem your ideal client has, but *what is the most immediate problem, the most immediate issue or crisis that they need to have solved, like, yesterday?* Because when you know what this is, you can speak to what's top of mind for them right at the moment.

The result that you can help them achieve, the long-term result, is an extension of this. *But what is the most immediate thing that they need help with?* We ask this question for two reasons. The first is that when you're talking with a prospective client, the issue they emphasize may or may not be the actual issue they're dealing with. To use myself as an example, oftentimes clients come to me because they need help with running social media ads. However, when I dig deeper, I often find that running social media ads isn't the problem at all. The real problem is that they need leads and clients, but don't have a way to achieve that. Once you're able to identify the problem that is top of mind for your ideal client, you're then able to recognize ideal clients based on the problems and language *they're already using*.

The second reason we ask this question is that it grants insight into your ideal client's priorities. When we talk about your offer, one of the things we talk about is how to help get your client immediate results. While you probably can't help them create long-term, sustainable transformation in the first week or two, chances are that you can help them get some quick wins to solve some of their most immediate issues.

What does your client want more than anything else in the world? What's their deepest desire? You can't speak to our ideal client's problems and fears without also speaking to their deepest desires—what they want more than anything else. When thinking about this question, try to be as specific as possible. For example, you might start with thinking that ideal client wants to be physically healthy. Instead of stopping there, dig a level deeper and envision some of the more specific scenarios that your ideal client wants. Do they want to be able to pick up their grandchildren? Do they want to run a marathon? Do they want to wake up each morning without feeling fatigued? Instead of coming up with abstract desires, get as concrete as you possibly can.

Next, pretend you're in your ideal client's situation—*what would you do if you were in their situation?* How would you solve the problem? You've already identified the steps that you would guide a client through to achieve that result, but it's also important to consider what *you* would do if you were in that situation. This slightly different angle to a similar question ensures that there's an alignment between what you would do yourself and what you would coach a client to do.

What's the biggest mistake your ideal client is making right now? This is probably one of the most important questions in this process because it's asking you to consider all the things your ideal clients are doing (or not doing) that are keeping them from achieving their desired result. Are they binge-eating when they should be dieting? Are they running social media ads when they should be creating their offer first? What are the small, mundane things that they are doing wrong that are leading them to all this frustration that they are experiencing?

Finally, *who is your competition?* Who are the other people or businesses in your space that you consider either direct or indirect competition? A key part of understanding your ideal client is knowing who else is competing for their attention and dollars, and this knowledge helps you start to notice what your competition is doing, and, more importantly, what's working and what's not.

If you say that no one is doing the same thing that you are, that may be true. But if you think that means that you don't have any competition, you're dead wrong. Competition is not people who are doing the same thing as you; your competition is businesses or people who are competing for your ideal client's attention and dollars.

For example, my competition isn't just limited to other business coaches specializing in organic client attraction. In fact, those coaches are the last thing I think of when I consider my competition. My prospective clients themselves are an example of my competition, especially when they believe that they can DIY their client attraction process. All the blog articles and free resources out there are my competition because they're competing for my ideal client's attention (and remember to get specific about *which* blogs and free resources your ideal clients are following). My competition includes digital marketing agencies, Facebook ad specialists, even the marketing software platforms that my ideal clients are considering. Competition doesn't necessarily mean Target versus Walmart; competition is who's competing for your ideal client's time, attention, and dollars.

IDEAL CLIENT QUESTIONNAIRE

What is the biggest result you can help a business or person achieve?

Describe the best client you've ever had. What were they like? What did they need? Why were they your favorite?

What is the single biggest problem your ideal client has?

What frustrates your ideal client more than anything else in the world?

What are the 3-5 steps they need to take for them to achieve their desired result?

What keeps your ideal client up at night? What are their deepest desires, anxieties, and frustrations?

What does your ideal client want to avoid at all costs (an event or occurrence that would leave them humiliated)?

What is the most immediate issue/crisis that they need to have solved right now?

What are the most mundane aspects of their day that frustrate them beyond belief?

What does your ideal client want more than anything else in the world? What is their deepest desire?

Step into your ideal clients' shoes. If you were in their situation, how would you solve the issue at hand?

What is the biggest mistake your ideal client is making right at this very moment?

Once you have worked through these questions, set them aside and do something else—take a walk, make some tea, whatever you need to do to shift your focus elsewhere.

Then, once you've taken a break and feel refreshed, come back to these questions, and expand on each of your answers with a focus on offering specific examples and imagery to illustrate what your ideal client's life looks like in their current situation. Don't just say that they're not satisfied with their job—show me what their behavior at work looks like, what's going through their mind, how it affects their home life.

The more specific you are, the better able you'll be to create content and messaging that speaks directly to your ideal clients.

Most coaches truly can help anybody—that's one of the beautiful things about coaching—but that doesn't mean it's a good idea to try to speak and appeal to everybody.

This is your niche—the specific group of people you are focused on helping, and whom the majority of your messaging and content is geared towards.

It doesn't mean that you have to turn away clients who fall outside your niche, or even that your hyper-focused messaging won't resonate deeply with hundreds of people outside your niche.

It's easy to view niching down as a limiting act—an action that's going to appeal to fewer people—but the reality is that the more you niche down, the more potent your messaging will become. And much like your offer and ideal client, your niche isn't a one-time decision that dictates the future of your life and business. Not satisfied with your niche? Make a shift. Your niche, like every other part of your business, evolves alongside you.

YOUR OFFER

Similar to not understanding my ideal client, I also didn't have a solid offer until I was several years into my business. I was making sales, but it was such a lengthy process that involved meeting a prospect, writing a proposal, answering questions about the proposal, and then finally making the sale. Writing the proposal alone lengthened my sales process dramatically, given that it would take a week to put it together while still juggling work for my other clients. And the idea of working on proposals for two different clients at the same time? No thank you.

This sales process wasn't just ineffective, it was inherently broken. It dramatically limited the number of clients I could bring on each month and took time away from actually working with clients. It also meant that whenever I didn't successfully make a sale with a prospect, I had already spent as much as five unpaid hours putting together that proposal for them. The biggest problem, though, was that it absolutely destroyed a prospect's momentum and excitement to work together.

Here's what the end of my sales conversations looked like:

> **Prospect:** *So, what does it look like to work together?*

> **Coach:** *Let me go put together a proposal for you, and then we can go from there.*

After a while, I started to notice that while prospects seemed excited to get started during our initial conversation, they seemed much more subdued and much less energized around working together than they had previously been.

Crafting a more detailed offer, however, allowed me to conduct that initial conversation much more effectively, which dramatically improved my conversion rate—all because I didn't let my prospect lose momentum:

> **Coach:** *Would you like for me to share what it would look like to work together?*
>
> **Prospect:** *Yes, please!*
>
> **Coach:** *Great! Here's exactly what it looks like to work with me, what it includes, and how it will help you achieve x (goal). We can go ahead and get started as soon as you're ready.*

Because I had a clearly defined, repeatable offer that I could present to my prospect, I could completely remove the proposal-writing step from my sales process and double my conversion rate at the same time.

The concern that I often hear at this point is about customization—the fear of losing the flexibility that comes with writing custom proposals for each of your prospects. That's a valid concern, likely informed by the fact that you know that no matter how clearly you define your ideal client, the particular details of their needs will sometimes differ.

Your clients' needs will indeed differ, sometimes slightly, and other times more dramatically, and that's perfectly fine—to be expected, even. The purpose of an offer is not to force your prospects into a box, but rather to create a framework that you can work within to serve your clients to the best of your ability. One way to think about your offer in this context is as a skeleton outline that serves as the "bones" of your offer. Then, as you talk with different prospective clients whose needs may differ, how you fill in that outline is the customization by which you put the "meat" onto that skeleton. Therefore, no matter how your prospects' needs differ, your process of working with them maintains the same general structure.

When building an offer, there are three primary components to think through, each of which plays an important role in your client attraction and sales processes: the result you can help someone achieve; why that result is important in the first place; and how you're going to help them get that result. But you can't have just a vague idea of what these things are. Just like in the process of uncovering more about your ideal client, one of the keys to crafting an offer is to be specific and concrete.

Let's look at an example:

Offer A: "I offer life coaching."

Offer B: "I help burnt out professional women rediscover themselves and create a life that energizes them and brings them joy."

If you were a burnt-out professional woman, which of those two offers would you be likelier to spring for? Offer B, right?

When thinking about what they need, most burnt out professional women don't envision themselves needing a life coach. But a chance to rediscover themselves, get energized, and find joy? Yes, please. Offer B focuses on the result (the greatly enhanced life), not the process (life coaching). Your clients care more about *what* you can help them achieve, rather than *how* you help them achieve it.

A couple of years ago I was working with Steve, a health and fitness coach who was struggling to bring new clients into his new flagship program designed to help older adults take charge of their physical health as they aged. As Steve talked about his program, my gut reaction was disbelief that he wasn't enrolling clients left and right into what seemed even to me like a no-brainer offer. And I'm not even an older adult!

As we dug deeper into his offer, I asked him what the experience was like for the clients—how he actually delivered his program. "Well, every other month I re-launch the program and take a cohort of 10-15 clients through the program, which includes online content, group calls, and several 1:1 coaching sessions," he said.

"But you're not getting those 10-15 clients each time you re-launch the program, right?"

"Correct. I'm usually only getting one or two people into the program."

"Which means you're still on the hook to deliver the program to them—a group program that's designed to be profitable for 10-15 participants, not one or two?"

Together, we created a mind map of not only what his program looked like, but also what he was doing to enroll clients. Once we had a bright and colorful mind map, we took a step back and noticed two things. First, his program was incredibly well-thought-out and structured, but was ultimately over-structured to the point that it was restricting him from trusting his intuition to best serve his clients. Because he had every aspect of his offer planned out in excruciating detail—many of which arguably weren't that important in the first place—he wasn't allowing himself any flexibility to make adjustments or improve his program as he was taking clients through it.

Second, because he was launching his program every two months (while also managing his existing cohort of clients), he was giving himself only two weeks to promote and fill each cohort. This meant that instead of being able to enroll and begin working with new clients any day of the week, he was limiting himself to just a fraction of that.

In short, he was shooting himself in the foot. He was treating his offer as if it were carved in stone forever and all eternity, and it was getting in the way of not only how he was serving his clients, but also how he was enrolling clients.

Over the next weeks, we tweaked the delivery of his program so that he was able to enroll new clients 52 weeks out of the year—a massive increase from only being able to enroll clients 12 weeks out of the year. By adjusting how he was delivering the program, he created *so* much more flexibility both for himself and for his clients, which meant that he was much better able to serve them.

With that newfound flexibility, he increased his conversion rate dramatically because he wasn't attempting to fit prospective clients into the narrow box that was the previous iteration of his program.

This is a prime example of Steve embracing the concept of *the evolving offer*—the practice of creating and selling an offer that you are always going to be improving, changing, and evolving. This is especially important when you're just starting out with a new offer because it means that in order to sell your offer, all you need to do is identify the transformation you're helping your clients achieve and the high-level steps you're going to take them through to achieve it.

That means we're not obsessing over the specifics like the number of 1:1 calls, number of group calls, or the clients-only Facebook Group. It's important to have some understanding of that, but at the end of the day, those specifics are always going to be changing and evolving.

That high-level stuff, though? That's pretty much going to stay the same. You'll tweak it as you go, but it's the delivery of the offer that's always going to be evolving so that you can help your clients get the best results.

We take this approach to do two things. First, we want to start getting clients quickly. We want to get people in the door, making sure that you have the tools to deliver the offer but knowing that the way you deliver the offer is going to change as you take on more clients and grow. Second, we want to put the clients first. Your top priority is always the client—helping your client get results. That means that for your first few clients, you're probably going to be doing more 1:1 coaching than anything else.

The reason you're likely going to start out with mostly 1:1 coaching is that it is an opportunity to get even clearer on what they need—and to give it to them. In theory, you could create a ton of pre-recorded content. But what happens time and time again is that one of the following situations occurs:

1. You pour time, energy, and money into creating that online training portal...and then don't make a single sale because the offer or the messaging wasn't tuned into what your ideal client needs at that point.
2. You do bring on a new client, and then in the first weeks of working with them realize that all the content you created for them *isn't actually what they need.* And you can't just force that content down their gullet anyway, because if it's not what they need it's not going to help them get results. In fact, it may hinder their ability to get results.

These two situations can both be prevented by *validating your offer first.* What we mean by validating your offer is making a sale—taking a credit card number and getting a new client. You might think that the first thing you need to do is market research, but each strategy session you have, each prospective client you talk to, *anyone you talk to who could be a prospective client*—that's your market research. You're not having those conversations solely to convert them to a new client; you're also having those conversations to continue to learn about your ideal client and hone in on your offer.

When you're creating a new offer, sure, be thinking about how you're going to fulfill it, but allow yourself some flexibility so that you can serve the client in the best way possible. But to start off, you probably want to put the emphasis on 1:1 coaching because if you're below $10k/month, it's not worth your time and energy to create that content. It's way more valuable to spend that time and energy attracting new clients and serving them on a more personal level.

To sell your offer, all you really need is clarity on the result you're going to help them achieve and the process you're going to take them through to achieve it. That's it—a skeleton outline that you can then customize for each client.

Don't worry, though—if you don't want to exclusively be doing 1:1 coaching for the rest of your life, you don't have to. As you begin to take on more clients, you learn even more about your ideal client—it's the process of continually conducting market research, learning and hearing what people are actually saying so that you can give them exactly what they need.

As you get even clearer about who your ideal client is, and as you begin to validate your offer over and over again (i.e., making sales), you can do less tailoring—and even less 1:1, if you want—because your offer is so dialed in.

CREATING YOUR OFFER

Now that you understand the foundational components of designing an irresistible offer, it's time to start putting the pieces together to create your offer. Below are ten questions to think through that will help you further hone in on your offer. And remember—don't worry too much about the logistics and nitty-gritty details quite yet. We'll get to those later.

Describe your client's current situation. Consider all the aspects of where your ideal client currently is—what are they dealing with, how is it affecting them? This is an excellent spot to envision *exactly* where your client is right now.

What is it costing them to stay where they are (financially, emotionally, physically)? In light of your ideal client's current situation—which you just identified—what is the cost of staying in that situation? Is there a monetary cost? An emotional cost? A physical cost?

What is the #1 most important thing they want to accomplish? You now know what your ideal client's current situation is, but where do they *want* to be? What's their goal? Where do they envision themselves?

What are the 4-5 steps you're going to walk them through to achieve that result? Your ideal client comes up to you and says, "Alright, I'm ready to get started." What do you do? Over the course of working with that client, what are the four or five major steps that you're going to walk them through?

How long would it take an average person to reach that result? What factors determine how quickly someone would achieve that result?

Over the course of working with you, how long do you suspect it would take a client to reach that #1 most important thing that you identified above? Beyond how long it would take the average person, consider what factors—perhaps dedication, consistency, etc. —would help someone reach their goal sooner (or later).

How important is the problem at hand? Why is it important? A client isn't going to pay thousands of dollars to solve a problem if it isn't an important problem. If it's not an important problem, chances are they'd be decently satisfied with a cheaper and likely less effective solution—whether it actually solved the problem at hand. Therefore, consider how important it is to address their current situation—and *why* it's important to address it.

How urgently do they want to solve the problem at hand? How quickly can you solve it? If a problem is important, then chances are that there's some amount of urgency attached to it. Understanding and addressing this urgency is one factor that will help make your offer irresistible because your client doesn't just want results, they want results *now*. At the same time, the problem is likely a complex one, meaning that solving it in its entirety within a matter of days or weeks is simply impossible; and if that's the case, it would be gross malpractice to claim otherwise. Therefore, a key to addressing your ideal clients' urgency is to identify which *specific* aspects of the problem you can help them solve in a matter of days or weeks. In other words, what are the quick wins you can help them achieve in the first days or weeks of working with you?

How sophisticated is the problem at hand? How certain are you that you can solve it? In the same vein as the problem's importance and urgency is its sophistication. As we mentioned above, the problem is likely fairly complex, but how complex is it? When a problem is sophisticated, it means that your ideal client has likely already tried several (and likely cheaper) solutions with little to no results. Solving a sophisticated problem ultimately makes you and your offer even more valuable.

What has your ideal client already tried to address their current situation? What makes your approach different, unique, or better? It's safe to assume that your ideal client has tried *something* to address the problem at hand. What is it they've tried, and why hasn't it worked for them in the past?

Describe what you do in one concise sentence that anybody can understand. Go ahead and give it a shot. Now that you've thought through these foundational aspects of your offer, try summing it up in one sentence. Don't worry about getting it perfect quite yet—you'll have plenty of time to massage the phrasing later on—so just focus on getting something down on paper.

OFFER CREATION QUESTIONNAIRE

What is your ideal client's current situation?

What is it costing them to stay where they are (financially, emotionally, physically)?

What is the #1 most important thing they want to accomplish?

What are the 4-5 steps you're going to walk them through to achieve that result?

How long would it take an average person to reach that result?

What factors determine how quickly someone would achieve that result?

How important is the problem at hand? Why is it important?

How urgently do they want to solve the problem at hand? How quickly can you solve it?

How sophisticated is the problem at hand? How certain are you that you can solve it?

What has your ideal client already tried to address their current situation? What makes your approach different, unique, or better?

How can you describe what you do in one concise sentence that anybody can understand?

Once you've answered these questions about your offer, do the same thing that you did when identifying your ideal client: Go take a break.

When you come back, take a look specifically at your answer to the above question, where you identified the 4-5 steps you would walk a client through to achieve their desired result. This is your process—this will become the clearest articulation of exactly what you help your clients achieve and how you do it.

Lost? Let me give you an example. Here's the four-step process I take my clients through. Notice how I name a specific result in each one and how, when you read them, you know *exactly* what I'm talking about:

1. First, we take an in-depth look at your business and learn it inside and out, and we use our findings to create a custom 12-week action plan that outlines exactly what we're going to do each week and how it gets you closer to your target revenue.

2. Then, we're going to create or fine-tune your offer and messaging so you can speak directly to your ideal clients' deepest desires and get them to raise their hands to work with you.

3. Once we have that foundational piece, we're going to leverage the latest organic social media techniques to connect with your ideal clients, build relationships, and book calls to talk about your offer.

4. Finally, we're going to turn our focus to helping you close more sales and sell effectively and authentically, so you can convert more of your calls into clients.

Say that you're on a call with me, and I've just shared those four steps with you. And say that you talked with someone else later in the day who said, "Yeah, I can help you get more clients," but didn't give you any insight into their process.

Who are you going to work with?

I'm going to continue using myself as an example here and say that when I work with clients, those steps (specifically the last three) can vary dramatically from person to person. Some of my clients need to focus their energy on LinkedIn, while others need to leverage Facebook or Instagram. Some clients need to work hard to beef up their content creation skills, while others can sit down and write a kick-ass social post without breaking a sweat.

People are different. People have different situations. People have different needs. And your clients are no exception. That's why your process needs to be specific enough to help your prospects understand what it looks like to work with you, but high-level enough that you're able to customize your offer to fit their needs.

That's why I say that I'm going to help my clients "leverage the latest organic social media techniques" rather than "use *x*, *y*, and *z* specific tactics on Facebook." Because what social platform my clients use varies, as does what they're actually *doing* on that platform and where they're focusing their energy.

Your offer and process are a skeleton outline, a coloring page that you can reproduce over and over again and simply color in the lines for each client.

PRICING

And now it's time for the inevitable question, the one that everyone asks at this point: *How do I price my offer?*

Glad you asked.

You'll notice that we've not yet talked about the actual deliverables of your program...how many sessions, whether it's group or 1:1 coaching, what kind of support you offer in between calls. But we're going to go ahead and talk about pricing anyway. That's because when pricing your offer, it's important to base it on the value your clients receive and the value of their results...*not on how many hours you spend on 1:1 coaching calls with them.*

In the same vein, it's why I recommend against working with new clients on a month-to-month basis, wherein they pay for a month of coaching and then may or may not continue the next month—because chances are slim that your clients will achieve truly sustainable and life-changing results in only four weeks. Offering three- or six-month packages, then, is usually the sweet spot that creates the space for lasting change.

These are the two main components you want to keep in mind when pricing your offer: the value of the results your clients achieve and the length of the program.

The latter component is significantly easier to tackle. A six-month coaching package should cost roughly double what your three-month package costs. Easy.

The more complex consideration, though, is pricing your offer based on the results your clients achieve while working with you. The easiest way to start this process is by identifying how your program helps your clients either make or save money. Value is most commonly thought of in dollar amounts, which makes pricing your offer easier when it helps people make or save money.

For example, a $5,000 offer might sound like a lot, but if it helps you make $100,000/year, it becomes a no-brainer.

Similarly, a $3,000 offer might seem overpriced, but if it helps you improve your health and avoid monstrous hospital bills, it's a no-brainer.

It's not just about making or saving money, though. Whatever situation your client is in right now, *there is a cost for doing nothing.* Whether it's in money that they could be making but aren't or hospital bills that are starting to accumulate, it is costing them to do nothing. Additionally, that cost almost inevitably will increase over time, meaning that the longer they remain paralyzed and don't act, the more it will ultimately end up costing them.

Of course, we know that value doesn't have to be associated with a dollar amount and oftentimes doesn't have anything to do with financial benefits (otherwise, nobody would ever have children, which are notoriously expensive).

Value comes in so many forms, so here are some questions to help you identify all the different types of value that your offer creates:

- How does your offer help save or create more time?
- How does your offer help strengthen their relationships?
- How does your offer help improve their mental health?
- How does your offer help improve their physical health?
- How does your offer help reduce stress?
- How does your offer help them sleep better at night?
- How does your offer help their social life?
- How does your offer make them more productive?
- How will your offer help them get the result or transformation faster than working on their own or trying other methods/solutions?

Identifying all the ways that your offer creates value for your clients is helpful when it comes to setting your price, but it also has many other benefits that show up throughout the entire process of attracting new clients:

It helps you align your messaging. When your messaging is fine-tuned to the point where you can speak directly to your ideal clients and their needs, your offer's value expands to address other aspects of your prospects' lives—not just within the specific area that you're helping them with.

You can create better content. In the same vein, you'll have the opportunity to create content that speaks to a person as a whole rather than to one specific issue or aspect of their identity. At the end of the day, everyone just wants to feel seen and understood, and the content you put out into the world is a massively effective tool for creating that feeling in your prospects.

You'll be able to talk more confidently about your offer. Knowing that your offer helps your clients achieve remarkable results in a plethora of different areas makes it ten times easier for you to talk about it—and its pricing—with confidence. There's a difference between talking about an overpriced offer and talking about a high-priced offer that's worth the money. Being clear on your offer's value ensures that you fall into the latter category every time.

YOUR PACKAGING

Now that you have a high-level understanding of your offer, it's time to begin thinking through how you're actually going to fulfill—or package—that offer. Just like everything else up to this point, *it's not going to be set in stone.* Nor should it be.

In other words, there's no use trying to get it perfect the first time. Because you won't. Instead, focus on making it the best you can, knowing that for every client or cohort you work with, you'll be making adjustments for the future. Remember, *every* single client is a guinea pig for future clients.

The first question to ask at this point is, "How quickly can I help a client achieve that massive result?" When your client needs a problem solved, they don't need it solved in a year—they need it solved now. Sure, you might not be able to help a client achieve a state of enlightenment in 12 weeks, but chances are that you can help them wake up every day more relaxed, energized, and satisfied. And 99% of the time, *that's the result that your clients want*—feeling relaxed, energized, and satisfied—not achieving a state of enlightenment.

The second question to ask is, "How do I fulfill the offer?" The sheer number of ways you can fulfill it can be overwhelming.

Should you do 1:1 or group coaching? Group mastermind? Online content? Facebook Group?

To break it down a little further, there are three primary ways that you can engage with your clients:

1. **1:1:** One-on-one coaching with your clients

2. **Group:** Coaching a group of people together

3. **Training:** Online course-like content that explains key concepts or principles (not a replacement for coaching, but rather an enhancement to a coaching program)

1:1 Coaching is what most people associate with being coached, but there are many different ways that 1:1 coaching can look:

- **Coaching sessions either in-person or virtually.** It's easy to default to a 60-minute session, but 30, 45, and 90-minute sessions are also great options, depending on what's best for your clients.
- **Support via text or instant message.** Even if it takes you 12-24 hours to respond to a client's question via instant message, the fact that your clients can reach you instantly can add so much value to your offer (consider it to be a priority lane for accessing you). Doing this, of course, requires that you have healthy boundaries—commit to only responding to support messages during the workday, for example.
- **Check-ins.** On the flip side, if you meet with a client every week or every other week, a quick "How're things going?" between sessions is a great form of 1:1 coaching.

Countless entrepreneurs are shifting to **Group Coaching** because it's commonly believed that you can't scale past $10-15k months if you're only doing 1:1. That's not true at all—you can do whatever works best for you and your clients.

Group coaching can indeed be an effective way to serve your clients. Here are two of the common ways you can incorporate group coaching into your offer:

- **Group coaching sessions.** The most common practice for group coaching sessions is to dedicate a certain amount of time to each participant. For example, if there are 6 participants in your 90-minute group coaching session, you'd dedicate roughly 15 minutes to each one. The primary benefit to a group session is that participants get answers to questions they might not have thought to ask, and participants benefit from other participants' presence— not just the coach's.[1]

- **Online community.** There are now a billion different platforms that you can host an online community on— Facebook being the most popular—but the core of it remains around creating an online space where participants can engage with and support one another. The most common types of engagement in online communities like these are sharing successes with the group, asking for advice, and offering support.

1: One of the key considerations around group coaching is the size of the group. Experiment with different group sizes and find what works best for you and your clients.

If part of your program requires that clients have an understanding of key principles or concepts, then adding a **training** component to your coaching program is a great way to communicate those concepts and to save you from repeating the same concepts over and over. This usually takes the form of an online training portal with content similar to what you might see in an online course. However, it's important to remember that while your training portal is important, it's absolutely not a replacement for 1:1 or group coaching. Nor is it a form of coaching at all, for that matter—it's a *teaching* tool.

One of the beautiful things about using a training portal as part of your coaching program is that *you don't have to create the entire portal before you can sell your offer.* Instead of trying to build out and record all the lessons immediately, just create your first module and then create the rest as your clients get to the point where they need them.

For example, if you have a 12-week coaching program and want to have a training module for each week, don't bust your ass creating twelve weeks' worth of content before you focus on *selling the coaching offer in the first place.* Instead, just create the first week's module, and while your client is working through Week 1, build out the second week's module.

It's a much easier way to go about things, for sure, but there are other significant benefits:

- It dramatically reduces the time it takes to get your offer to market. Instead of waiting to make sales until you have the entire program built out, you can go ahead and make sales immediately.

- The trainings that you think you need to create might not actually be what your clients need. Countless times, I've seen coaches build out their training modules, only to find with their first client that *they built the wrong ones.* So, they're left to redo all the work that they could have done just once.

- You actually get paid upfront for the work it takes to build out a training portal. Rather than creating everything with the *hope* that you'll bring in a client for your program, you only create the modules once you have the money in the bank.

To help you visualize what a training portal could look like for your coaching program, here are a few examples:

- **Life coaching.** Goal setting, progress tracking, and journal prompts.
- **Fitness coaching.** Videos of stretches, exercise routines, or workout plans.
- **Business coaching.** Important business concepts, explanations of tactics.

If a training portal makes sense for your clients, go for it. But if you're unclear on the value that it would provide your clients, come back to it as an option for the future. And remember, the training portal is not a replacement for coaching; otherwise, you're just selling another online course.

WHERE TO BEGIN

Packaging your offer is not the process of figuring out how many components you can jam into an 8, 10, or 12-week program. Rather, it is the process of determining *the best way you can help your clients achieve their results.*

Remember those 4-5 steps you identified that you're going to take your ideal client through? Let's start there.

Take a look at each of those steps you listed, and for each one, answer this simple question:

What is the best way to walk a client through this step?

For example, let's take a look at what this could look like for a business coach:

Step 1: Help the client identify their business goals and create an action plan to get there.

The best way to fulfill this step would be through 1:1 coaching.

Step 2: Create and implement a system for consistent lead generation.

The best way to communicate the concepts and processes is through an online training portal; the best way to guide them through the implementation process is with group coaching calls.

Step 3: Convert a higher percentage of their leads into customers or clients.

The best way to help a client increase their conversion rate would be a combination of group and 1:1 coaching calls plus an online community for group support.

Step 4: Optimize their systems and processes for sustainable growth and scale.

The best way to guide a client through optimizing their systems would be through a group mastermind.

You'll notice that the most important question we're asking here is, "What's best for the client?" And while it might be easy to take a look at your offer as a whole and say, "Oh, this is a 1:1 offer," or, "This is purely a group offer," that's not what we're doing here.

Rather than assigning one mode of coaching to the entire offer, we're breaking the offer down step-by-step and identifying *the best way to deliver each individual step.*

For any new offer, start small at first—using mostly 1:1 coaching with perhaps some group calls here and there. But as you get more dialed in to your clients' pain points, you'll start to see opportunities for how you can serve your clients even more powerfully.

GET EVEN MORE GRANULAR

This step is somewhat optional, but I highly recommend it because it gives you *even more clarity* on how you're going to work with clients—down to the nitty-gritty logistics of exactly how you deliver each step.

Take the steps and delivery mechanisms you worked with above. For each step, you're going to identify two things—what *you're* going to do in that step, and what the *client* is going to do in that step. The concept of dividing out what you are going to do and what they are going to do applies no matter what kind of business you are in—and while this works best for service-based businesses, it also works well for any type of business. For example, if you have an eCommerce business, you (the seller/merchant) have to do something to fulfill the order, and when they (the customer) receive it, they have to do something to get value out of it, whether that's consuming content or using the product.

To give you a sense of what this looks like in practice, I'm going to use my coaching program as an example. In a nutshell, I help small businesses create a systematized online marketing process that a) drives traffic, b) generates leads, and c) converts clients. I help small businesses generate a massive amount of warm, qualified leads.

This is my five-step process:

1. I audit their business's current marketing efforts and put together a 12-week action plan that will help them reach their goals.
2. I teach and help them implement my proven organic traffic system so they can consistently drive awareness and engagement.
3. I teach them about lead generation and coach them to develop their own system so they can turn a healthy percentage of traffic into leads.

4. I coach them on creating effective email and content to build trust and relationships while converting more clients.

5. I give them concrete strategies and best practices for increasing both immediate and lifetime client value (i.e., retaining customers) and for collecting and leveraging social proof.

If we take the first step and break it down into two pieces—what *I, the coach* am going to do and what *they, the client* are going to do, it looks like this:

What I Do: I perform a marketing audit/assessment. To achieve that, I review and log findings from all of their outward facing marketing assets, review responses from their onboarding questionnaire, and review my notes from previous conversations with them. Then, I custom design a 12-week action plan for the client. I identify the client's priorities and objectives, break them down into a 12-week plan, and assign action steps for each week.

What They Do: Complete the onboarding questionnaire and send me a link to their website and their social media profiles.

It's pretty simple, right? It's just broken down into who does what so that you can articulate to clients what it looks like to work with you. Sure, you probably won't give a prospective client all the nitty gritty details during the sales process, but it creates confidence in your clients when you're able to show them a clear process that will take them from where they are now to where they want to be.

If you are having a hard time figuring out what the concrete things are that you need to do and that they need to do, picture what you would tell a client in this situation. And don't overthink it. It's perfectly fine to say a "meeting or a Zoom call where we talk about your progress over the past week, dig into any obstacles that came up, and make a game plan for the next week." As long as you can confidently explain the process you take your clients through, you've got it.

YOUR MESSAGING

As I was growing up, my father was a pastor, which meant that a considerable part of my childhood was spent in and around the church. As a result, I grew up with a pretty decent vocabulary and understanding of Christian beliefs. But there was one phrase in particular that everyone kept saying, but no one seemed to understand what it actually meant—the "Holy Spirit." I asked my dad at some point what the Holy Spirit was, and the fact that I don't remember his response is a pretty good indicator that his answer wasn't clear and concrete enough for a young child's brain.

If you want to stump almost any Christian, ask them what the Holy Spirit is. They'll probably pause for a minute, stumble through answering it, and whatever they say, it'll likely be a fairly vague response that doesn't actually tell you much. Yet, Christians refer to the Holy Spirit all the time—it's used in prayers, hymns, and even casual conversation ("The Holy Spirit was watching out for me there"). But no one seems to know what it actually means.

That's how a lot of entrepreneurs talk about "messaging." It's the word that everyone throws around, but most don't have a solid understanding of what it actually means; and if they do know what it means, their definition is likely different from the entrepreneur who's sitting right next to them. Key concepts like "offer" and "ideal client" have universally accepted definitions because they're much more concrete, and, in all honesty, self-explanatory. But messaging? Not so much.

Unlike the Holy Spirit, however, messaging can be defined without reigniting a centuries-old debate between theologians. In its simplest sense, *messaging is how you communicate your offer in a way that resonates with your ideal client.* Most entrepreneurs fixate on identifying their offer and ideal client—which is great, but the primary value in that is clarifying those two things *in your head.*

If you want to sell your offer, though (and you probably do want to), you have to communicate that offer. Your prospects must have the same understanding of your offer that you do. That's where your messaging comes in—the foundational tenets of how you talk about your offer. Your messaging shows up in every aspect of your client attraction process—in your content, copy, strategy sessions, and branding. It's the foundational element that makes it easy to decide whether to use one word or phrase over another and to choose which topic to write a social media post on.

It all comes back to messaging, and if you want your offer to resonate with your ideal client, then your job is to dial in your messaging to align with your offer and ideal client.

In this section, we're going to talk about how to bridge that gap between your offer and content by dialing in on your messaging. The two main aspects of this conversation are *content* and *messaging*, so it's worth defining what exactly we mean when we use those terms.

Content is what you put out into the world—anything that educates, entertains, or inspires. Social media updates, blog posts, emails, are all examples. We're going to dive way deeper into content later in this book, but for now, we're focusing on messaging.

Messaging is the language you use to create that content—it's the broader way that you communicate with your ideal clients.

When your content and messaging don't align, it might mean that the messaging you're using in your podcast is actually a little bit different than the messaging you're using in your social media post, which is a little bit different from the messaging you use in an email newsletter.

Your goal is to create a complete alignment, wherein your offer aligns with your messaging and your messaging aligns with your content.

There's a simple framework that will help you create that relationship, and the goal of this framework is simple: *Help your ideal clients see the mistakes they're making and problems they're having, show them the implications of that mistake or problem, show them the benefit of fixing it, and tell them what they need to do to fix that mistake.*

In a nutshell, you want to create a *mindset shift* for your ideal clients.

What mistakes are they making? What are the problems your ideal clients are having, and what mistakes are they making? Remember to get specific. The best mistakes and problems are often the most specific, concrete, (seemingly) mundane—the day-to-day mistakes that they aren't even thinking about.

What are the pains of making those mistakes and having those problems? What are the consequences of making that mistake—the consequences they might not even be experiencing yet, but will eventually? What frustrations arise from their making this mistake (that they don't even realize)?

What would be the benefits and results of solving those pain points? When they fix this mistake, what benefits and results do they experience? Upon getting those benefits and results, how does that affect every aspect of their life?

What do they need to do to resolve it? What are the high-level things they need to do to solve that problem and reap the benefits (what they need to do, not necessarily *how* they need to do it)?

Brainstorm as many mistakes and problems as you can, and for each one, identify the consequence, benefit of resolving it, and what they need to do to make that happen.

The best way to get started is to draw up a four-column table with these headings:

- Mistake or Problem
- Resulting Pain
- Benefits of Solving
- How to Resolve It

Then in the leftmost column, start brainstorming the mistakes your ideal clients are making and the problems they're having, and working left to right to dig into each of the components of that mistake or problem.

As with the work you've already done around your offer and ideal client, the more specific you can get with each one, the better. For example, if you're a life coach identifying problems that your ideal clients are facing, you might identify "not being able to get work done" as a problem.

Try to dig a little deeper, though. Are they having trouble sitting down and finding the motivation to get started (in which case it's a problem around motivation)? Or are they sitting down and getting started, but their attention starts to drift after ten minutes (in which case it's a problem around focus)? Are they dealing with both? Great, then those are two entirely different line items.

But if you want to get even more specific (and you should), then identify the concrete mistakes they're making that are creating those problems in the first place. Here are some examples of what those could be:

- They wake up, throw some clothes on, and sit down at the desk expecting to channel a fountain of productivity from the moment they wake up. In other words, they're not taking the time to fill their energy tank before getting started for the day.
- They're going to sleep too late and feel groggy and exhausted when they wake up in the morning.

- They're not planning out their weeks and days, so they don't have a clear idea of what they need to be focused on and when.
- They sit down to work, but keep their email in a corner of their screen and their phone within arm's reach. They're inundated with distractions the entire time.
- They are starting their workday by checking and responding to email, rather than focusing on the most important task of the day.

And you guessed it...all of those things would be excellent line items for this fictional life coach. The more specific you are when identifying the mistakes your ideal clients are making and the problems they're dealing with, the more dialed in your messaging will become. And the more dialed in your messaging is, the better and stronger you'll be able to connect with your ideal clients.

Try to fill out at least twenty rows of your messaging spreadsheet and treat it as a living document—always adding new mistakes/problems as they arise (because they will).

Then hold on to this document because it's going to be your guiding compass when we talk about creating content later in this book.

THE PROCESS

At this point, you have a strong understanding of the foundations of your coaching business: who your ideal client is, what you're offering, how you're packaging it, and how you're talking about it. These are the four elements of that foundation, upon which the rest of your client attraction strategy is built.

Now that you have that foundation, it's time to dig into the process itself. In the following sections, we are going to take a high-level look at each part and then break down each part of that process even further.

It's nearly impossible to understate the significance of the *process* by which you attract new clients. There are many processes for generating leads and bringing on new clients, and while we are focusing on one very specific process in this book, most entrepreneurs fail to have any sort of process in the first place.

Several years ago, I was talking with Micaela, a new client I was onboarding. As part of getting a solid understanding of her business, I asked her what her process was for getting new clients. "Well," she said, "I post on social media, I have a lead magnet and a landing page for that, and I send out emails to my list every now and again."

Well, that's not exactly a process. That's just an amalgamation of different actions. "What's the process, though? How do you get in front of new people, connect with them, and start conversations with them?"

"I just told you," she said, and I could start to hear the frustration in her voice. "I post on social media. I have a lead magnet. I have an email list."

I like to think that the next thing I said was, "Certainly, so the thing here is that that's not an actual process. For example, making a cake is a process. You have to mix the ingredients in a certain order, bake the cake, let it cool, and then decorate it. If you decorated the cake before you let it cool, it wouldn't turn out too well; or if you baked the cake before mixing the ingredients, you wouldn't even have a cake.

"A process is a recipe—it's a series of steps, one right after the other, wherein each step builds off what was done in the previous one. In your case, it sounds like you have the ingredients to bake the cake, but perhaps not the right recipe for putting those ingredients together to produce a cake. Would you say that's true?"

In reality, I think I said something more to the effect of, "Got it, that's definitely something we'll look at working together," and then proceeded to move on to my next question. Now I know better.

The point is that Micaela didn't have a process. She couldn't say to herself, "I need to make three sales this month; therefore, I need to follow this recipe to make that happen by the end of the month." Instead, she was haphazardly throwing together various ingredients hoping something—in this case new clients—would result.

But this is where things can be confusing, even misleading— *sometimes that works.* Occasionally you *do* get some amount of success from throwing shit together and seeing what happens. In fact, that's how most entrepreneurs get their first few clients. They put themselves out into the world and cross their fingers that someone will buy. *And that's great.* It's how I got my first few clients, and it's one of the most effective strategies for just getting started.

However, that approach doesn't work forever—call it beginner's luck, a stopgap measure, or whatever else, but it doesn't produce consistent, reliable results. For some entrepreneurs, that's fine. They're in the business to have fun, maybe a side hustle, and take what business that comes their way. For more proactive entrepreneurs ready to make $10k+ every month, though, it's not a sustainable solution. That's where the need for a process comes into play.

Simply having a process, however, isn't quite enough—it actually has to be an effective process that *works.*

More recently, I was working with Paige, a coach who had been working her ass off over the past 12 months to build her coaching business. When I asked her about her current process for attracting new clients, she immediately rattled off her step-by-step system for generating leads and bringing on new clients, complete with "First we do this, then we do that." She had the concept of a client attraction process down.

The only problem? It wasn't working. In the past 12 months, she had yet to enroll her first client into her signature coaching program. She had a process, just not one that was producing results for her.

It's not enough simply to have the ingredients to attract new clients—you need the *recipe* that helps you understand how and in what order those ingredients mix to achieve your result.

To begin, it's important to understand the difference between *strategy* and *tactics* because while these two words are often used interchangeably, they're actually quite different. Treating them as synonyms while reading this book will ultimately create massive confusion.

Strategy is the high-level overview of how you attract new clients.

Tactics are the things you actually do to attract new clients.

In other words, your strategy is *what* you need to do, and the tactics behind it are *how* you're going to do it. Without tactics, your strategy is just theory—because those tactics give the strategy legs to stand on.

For example, a strategic piece of advice would be "You need to build authority." That's a great piece of advice and is often true for many entrepreneurs, but you need tactics to build that authority. One tactic that fits under that strategy, then, would be to post on social media each day.

That's a solid tactic, but it doesn't quite go far enough to be very effective. That's because there are various levels to marketing tactics, and if your high-level tactic is simply social media posts, you need to get more specific. In this case, there are some important questions to answer so that you can best leverage that tactic:

- What social media platforms should you post to?
- How long should your posts be?
- How often should you post?
- What type of content should you create?
- What will you share?
- How often will you share it?
- What hashtags should you use with each post?

Each of these questions is a tactical decision in and of itself. And there are *tons* more that we could go into, but the point is that if you don't spend the time answering these questions, then your larger strategy will fall flat.

BUILDER AND DRIVER TASKS

When it comes to growing your business, there are two types of tasks: *builder tasks* and *driver tasks. Understanding these two types of tasks will help you effectively choose which tactics to pursue and which to save for later.*

Builder tasks are precisely what they sound like. These are things that don't necessarily drive immediate client attraction results but work longer term for you—tasks that are part of building a long-term business. Examples of these tasks are lead magnets, landing pages, email sequences, building a website, writing blog articles, optimizing your website for search engine results (SEO). The major advantage of builder tasks is that they help you more effectively leverage your time.

These tasks have massive potential to generate results, but in the longer term. Therefore, the downside is that they don't immediately bring in new clients. And if you're a newer entrepreneur, you can't depend solely on these tasks because you need clients in the next couple of weeks and months—not six, nine, or even twelve months down the road.

That brings us to the second type of task, *driver tasks*. These are the tasks that drive you forward in a much more immediate way, propelling you towards getting clients sooner rather than later. These tasks function under the simple philosophy that the quickest and most efficient way to attract new clients is to connect with them on a personal level, have conversations with them about your offer, and bring them on as clients if it's a good fit.

Examples of driver tasks include posting and engaging on your profile and in various groups and communities, starting conversations with prospects, and reaching out to prospects who previously were not a good fit. These are the tasks that produce much quicker results.

The downside of driver tasks, though, is that they are less scalable than builder tasks. While driver tasks are quite effective and can easily get you to $10-15k months, relying on them to get you beyond that is less reliable. That's because, as you build your audience, driver tasks become time-consuming to the point that they're simply not sustainable.

The success of your driver tasks is directly correlated to the amount of time you spend on them. If you spend an hour focused on booking five strategy sessions, for example, then it will take two hours to book ten. That's fine to get started, but when you move to scale your business beyond that and need to book five strategy sessions a day, that means you're spending five hours just on the booking side of things. Because builder tasks don't leverage time in the same way, they're excellent for scaling.

When talking about builder and driver tasks, one is not inherently better than the other—each has their place. If you are just getting started, you want to put most of your energy into those driver tasks, but that doesn't mean you want to ignore the builder tasks until you absolutely have to scale. Therefore, it becomes about splitting your energy between the two, which is often based on where you are in your business:

- If you are just getting started and are still trying to get that first client, you likely want to focus 100% on driver tasks.
- If you have brought on a few clients but are still struggling to create a *consistent* flow of new clients, then you likely want to focus roughly 90% of your energy on driver tasks and 10% on builder tasks.
- If you are consistently bringing on new clients and are moving towards having a booked schedule, then you want to spend less energy on driver tasks—something like 50% on each type of task.

- If lack of time is becoming a barrier to your client attraction process—you simply don't have the time for driver tasks because you are so booked up with clients—then this is the point where most of your energy should be poured into builder tasks.

The vast majority of coaches I encounter—and likely of the coaches reading this—find themselves neatly in one of the first two situations that I outlined above. Therefore, we'll primarily focus on driver tasks rather than builder tasks.

When I talk with new clients, one of the most common things I hear is, "I know I should be doing *xyz*, but I haven't done that yet." They're talking about all the things that they think they've been told they should be doing to grow their business—blogging, teaching webinars, launching a podcast, building a website. The list goes on. Most of the time, those "shoulds" are actually builder tasks, not driver tasks. So, when you find yourself feeling like you "should" be doing something but aren't, ask yourself whether this is something that's going to help you build a long-term business or drive more immediate results, and then treat it accordingly.

Driver tasks are all about starting new conversations and making your next sales, which means that they help you achieve much more immediate results than builder tasks. In addition to producing much quicker results, driver tasks position you to implement builder tasks by helping you gain a clearer understanding of your ideal client and the messaging that resonates with them.

What you learn in those conversations influences the types of blog articles you put out in the future, the types of keywords that you optimize for in the search engine optimization process. They're not totally unrelated, but you have to pay attention to where you're spending most of your energy and if that's appropriate for where you are in your business.

Because the truth is, I see so many people who are building these complex funnels, email sequences, dropping thousands of dollars on ads every month, and they are not getting any results. And that's because they are building a long-term business rather than trying to get that jumpstart, and that jumpstart is significant.

It's not just a matter of getting cash in the bank quickly. It's a matter of learning more about your ideal client. It's a matter of figuring out what your ideal clients actually want and need. It's the process of refining your offer. And once you have those three things, you will be much better positioned to do those builder tasks.

So, keep that distinction in mind and whenever you are doing anything in terms of working on your business, make sure that you're asking yourself, "Is this a driver task or is this a builder task?" and making sure it's appropriate for where you are in your business right now.

YOUR #1 PRIORITY

You may think that your #1 priority is to make $10,000 each month, but that's not a priority—that's your goal.

When we're setting revenue goals for our business, it's easy to say, "I want to make $10,000 next month." It's good to have that goal to work towards, but the problem with this type of goal is that it's a *lagging indicator*—which means that by the time you know whether you've hit your goal or not, it's too late to do anything about it. Because it'll be the end of the month.

Lagging indicators are the results of your effort—such as bringing on x number of clients or making $10,000. *Leading indicators*, in contrast, are the metrics that indicate whether you're going to reach your desired result.

In the context of your client attraction process, the primary leading indicators that dictate whether you reach your goal (the lagging indicator) are *how many conversations you have with prospective clients* (i.e., strategy sessions), and *how many of those conversations turn into sales* (i.e., your close rate). That means that to make $10,000 next month, you're going to reverse engineer the numbers so that you know exactly how many strategy sessions you need to conduct and how many of those you need to close in order to reach your sales goal.

Say your offer is $3,000, and you want to hit $10,000 next month. That means you need to make four sales at $3,000, which comes out to $12,000 ($2,000 over your goal, since $10,000 is not easily divisible by $3,000).

Four sales at $3,000 means four new clients. That's pretty basic math, but let's take it a level deeper, so we can identify exactly how many strategy sessions you need to have next month to reach that target.

Let's say you close 20% of the strategy sessions you conduct—not a great close rate, but not awful, either. That means that for every five strategy sessions you conduct, one of those becomes a client.

And if you need to make four sales at a 20% close rate, that means you need to conduct 20 strategy sessions over the course of next month. Given that there are roughly twenty workdays in a month, that evens out to one strategy session per day.

So, if you intend to make $12,000 next month, need to get started now on booking those calls so that when it rolls around, you already have calls lined up.

If you approach your client attraction game from that angle—focusing on the number of strategy sessions booked and the rate you close them—rather than fixating on the number of sales you need to make, that target goal of $10,000 becomes infinitely more achievable because *you have a clear path to get there.* You know exactly what you need to do to make that happen, which means that you're not sitting around hoping to get more clients. You're actively going out and getting them.

Fast-forward a month, and you've crushed your $10,000 goal and brought on four new clients for a total of $12,000 (congrats!). Where do you go from there? You *could* do the same thing all over again, *or* you could look at the different metrics and see how you can influence each of them to achieve the same (or better) results:

- Metric 1: The number of strategy sessions conducted. You can book even more strategy sessions. Easy.

- Metric 2: Your price point. If you raise your price point from $3,000 to $4,000, suddenly you only need three sales to hit $12,000, not four sales.
- Metric 3: Your close rate. If you elevate your sales skills and increase your 20% close rate to 40%, you need only half the strategy sessions to achieve the same results.

What happens when you increase all three of those metrics? That's where the most significant growth happens. You book 30 strategy sessions, raise your price point to $4,000, and increase your close rate to 40%. That's $48,000. Maybe you don't increase each of those metrics so significantly all at once, but when you do work towards improving each of them, your results start to multiply dramatically.

Instead of just saying, "I want to make $10,000 next month," reverse engineer those numbers so that you can know exactly what you need to do to make that happen—and then go do it.

YOUR CLIENT ATTRACTION PROCESS

Now that you know the basics, we can get started by first talking about the strategy side of things before diving into specific tactics.

There are five components to any successful client attraction process, and each is equally important. The good news is that they're fairly basic:

1. Finding where your ideal clients are
2. Connecting with your ideal clients

3. Booking calls with ideal clients who need your help
4. Closing sales with dream clients who are a good fit

We're going to start with a high-level overview of this part of the funnel—all the way from finding your ideal clients to getting them on a strategy session.

This piece of the funnel is arguably the most important because it is what results in strategy sessions, and, as you know, the number of quality strategy sessions you have directly correlates with the number of sales you make.

Before we get started, there are four important things to keep in mind:

First, this part of the process is all about starting natural, value-driven conversations with your clients that ultimately result in a conversation with them about your offer. Much like the rest of your client attraction process, this process depends on taking consistent daily action to build assets, which create massive results. The content you post, the conversations you start, and the engagements you do are all assets—all of which build momentum to get you closer to the next sale.

Second, this process is best viewed as a flywheel—a device that stores potential energy. It might start turning slowly at first, but when it takes off it uses all of that stored potential energy to turn rapidly. Getting this process going might feel slow and pointless—feeling more like a hamster on a wheel—but when you gain that momentum, you start to turn your walk into a jog, and then your jog into a full-fledged sprint.

Third, this process is a series of simple actions that flow naturally into one another. If it seems simple, that's because it is—and that's the beauty of it. Simple actions are good, but they don't do much if they're not connected to something bigger—the next action or the next piece of the puzzle. This strategy is a series of super simple tactics, strung together to create an effective client attraction process.

Fourth and finally, your mindset is everything, which means that how you show up to implement this process directly impacts the results you achieve. The biggest mindset shift to consider is that your focus in this process is not selling. Selling is part of it, which we'll talk about later, but as you're implementing this process, your focus is on *connecting and creating organic conversations*. Many people tend to view "organic traffic" as any traffic source that is not paid—anything that's not Facebook Ads, Google Ads, YouTube Ads, or any other advertising medium.

That's true to an extent, but it insinuates that "organic" simply means "not advertising," and that's not true. If we look at the word "organic" in its truest sense, it means natural, not forced, not altered chemically or otherwise. And *that's* what we're doing here—having natural conversations that build authentic relationships.

The next question, then, becomes why we're starting here in the first place. Why not one of the other millions of approaches you could be using to attract new clients? There are several reasons for this, the first being that the best way to determine whether your offer is viable is to sell it. Not to grow your email list or to get people to come to a webinar, but to take a credit card number over the phone and sell your offer. There are a lot of so-called vanity metrics that we could look at—the number of new email subscribers or attendees at a webinar—but the metric that really matters is the number of conversations you're having about your offer and the number of sales that you make. And this is the shortest route to that path.

This process not only validates your offer, but also gathers information about your ideal clients—learning more about them, and, more importantly, what resonates with them the most. And throughout that, you're building genuine relationships with your ideal clients—not superficial, distanced relationships, but actual relationships with real people.

At this point, you know that from a strategic perspective, your client attraction process looks like this:

As we've discussed, that's the *strategy* behind your client attraction process, and now it's time to look a little deeper at the *tactics* that give the strategy legs to stand on. We'll first take a look at the three core components of this strategy, and once you have a solid understanding of each of those, we'll discuss where and how each of them fit into the strategy I've outlined above.[2]

Component #1: Your Profile

The first major piece of your client attraction process is your social profile—whether that's on Facebook, LinkedIn, or Instagram—which we'll dive into more deeply later. Your profile is going to serve as a home base of sorts, as every engagement and conversation you have on social media will ultimately result in people viewing it. When you engage with someone, they'll likely click through to view your profile. When someone sees one of your posts and is interested in learning more about you, they'll click through to view your profile.

Your ideal clients are going to see your profile quite often, which means that it's important that it accurately and authentically represents you. To make this happen, there are several considerations when it comes to your profile.

The first is *profile optimization*, which refers to the process of ensuring that your profile as a whole aligns with your brand as a coach or consultant. These are the nitty gritty details like your

---

2: As we discuss these components, note that the specific terminology varies between social media platforms; for example, "Friends" on Facebook is equivalent to "Connections" on LinkedIn and "Followers" on Instagram. The same concepts apply to all three of these social media platforms, although the terminology of each platform varies slightly.

profile photo, bio, and any old photos from college that you'd rather your ideal clients not lay eyes on (it's fine, we all have them).

The second is your *profile content*, which is what you post on your profile. When someone visits your profile, they might take a quick glance at your photo and bio, but then quickly proceed to scroll through your most recent posts—and, of course, you want to make sure that they see the remarkable content you're putting out into the world.

The third is *profile engagement*, which is the engagement that's happening on your profile posts. The more engagement (likes, shares, and comments) that happens on any one post results in *even more people seeing that post*, which means that *even more people end up clicking through to your profile*. Therefore, you must engage with people who like, share, or comment on your profile posts so that you can create more traffic coming to your profile.

Component #2: Groups and Communities

Of course, you can post outstanding content on social media every day of the week, but if the only people who see it are already in your network, then you're not going to have much luck attracting clients on a consistent basis.

This is where groups and communities come in—you can find your ideal clients in the communities they're already a part of and connect with them. There are three main considerations here, each of which we'll dive into more fully later.

The first is *identifying groups and communities that contain your ideal client*. This is the process of figuring out where your ideal clients are already hanging out online and joining those communities yourself.

The second is *integrating yourself into those groups and communities*. This can look like joining in on the conversation via comments, adding value, and becoming a part of the community—not as a salesperson, but as a peer.

The third is *posting content in those groups and communities*—beyond engaging in existing conversations, actually starting your own conversations in those groups.

Component #3: Friends & Messages

The final main component of this part of the client attraction process is bringing people from those groups and communities into your network and starting conversations with them. There are two main pieces to this: expanding your friends/connection list and starting a direct message (DM) conversation with them.

First, you're growing your friends list by leveraging the groups and communities you're in, followed by continuing the conversation with them beyond the engagement you had with them in that group.

This is where the question of your mindset—showing up from a place of connection rather than sales—becomes even more important. Your main priority in this step is to build rapport in these conversations, unearth their challenges and pains, and ultimately see if they're a good fit for your offer.

Now that we've looked at the three main components of this part of the client attraction process, let's look at how these pieces fit together to form a simple funnel for finding your ideal clients, connecting with them, and getting them on a strategy session:

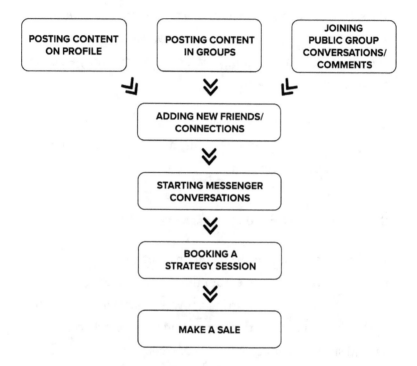

As you can see by looking at the top half of the funnel, the top four levels each play a distinct role in getting you closer to a sale. To simplify it, this entire process boils down to five main steps:

- Creating and posting content to your profile and to groups that contain your ideal client
- Having public conversations in the comments section of posts

- Connecting with/adding people you interact with in posts & comments
- Starting private conversations with new friends/ connections
- Turning private conversations into strategy sessions

If that feels overwhelming, don't worry—we're going to tackle each one in much deeper detail and break down the process into manageable chunks.

WHAT YOU NEED TO CREATE SUCCESS

Having worked with hundreds of clients to successfully implement this client attraction process, it's easy at this point for me to identify the most common pitfalls and obstacles that you'll likely experience. Fortunately, these pitfalls and obstacles don't have to stand in the way of consistently attracting your ideal clients, and there are only three things you need to create massive results: *consistency, flexibility,* and *excitement.*

In this context, *consistency* means taking a series of small, imperfect actions every day. None of the actions you're going to take in this process is massive in and of itself. They are simple and small; that's because taking massive action every day is impossible to do consistently, but that's okay because consistent small actions add up to produce more results than inconsistent massive actions do. Sure, you might be able to take massive action every day for a couple of weeks, but what happens after that? Taking smaller, more bite-sized action is infinitely more manageable and sustainable, which ultimately helps you maintain consistency.

The second thing you need is *flexibility*, which means the ability to adapt and change your strategy as needed. When done in its entirety, the client attraction process you're learning in this book *will* produce results. At the same time, individual aspects of this strategy will work better for you than others—and that's because your personality, niche, and offer all influence what works best for your business. Therefore, pay attention to what concrete actions are getting the best results for you and do more of those. On the flip side, pay attention to what concrete actions are getting the least results, and experiment to adapt them to fit *your* business. Even though this is the most effective client attraction process out there for coaches today, your success depends in large part on your intuition and ability to adapt it for your unique business.

Finally, you need *excitement*. Some aspects of this strategy will seem more thrilling and energizing than others, but it's important to bring the same level of excitement to every part of the process. You will experience by far the best results when you approach your client attraction with excitement and energy, not only about the results you're working toward but also about the process itself. Finding this excitement can look very different from person to person, but strategies to bring excitement to your everyday client attraction tasks can include having a clear motivation for your intended outcome, visualizing that outcome, and adapting the process to be more enjoyable and exciting for you. At the end of the day, it comes down to how you play the game, and the more excited you are about the game, the better your results will be.

FINDING YOUR IDEAL CLIENTS

I'VE ALWAYS BEEN A CONTENT POWERHOUSE, meaning that I can produce content all day long until my fingers start to bleed. I can write like a motherfucker, appear (somewhat) charming on camera, and deliver an excellent podcast interview—all without breaking a sweat.

In the past year alone I've been interviewed on 15 different podcasts, produced over 35 hours of video content, and written over 200,000 words of content. In other words, if content is king, then I'm the queen.

So, when I started doing this whole marketing thing, you can imagine that I felt pretty confident when I heard every marketing guru out there saying that "If you put quality content out there, your ideal client will come to you."

Honestly? After considering that piece of convenient advice to be my primary client attraction tool for a couple of years, I've come to this groundbreaking conclusion: It's bullshit. Sure, there's some amount of truth to that statement, but when it comes to attracting coaching clients, it's mostly false.

It assumes that your ideal clients are looking for you in the first place. Specifically with coaching, most people who fit your ideal client profile aren't out there actively looking for a coach. In fact, they might not have even considered a coach as a solution to their problem and are instead stuck reading various self-help books, trying to do it alone with little to no success.

Even if your ideal client *is* out there looking for coaching, chances are slim that they're going to find you if they don't already know who you are. If they do a Google search for anything related to coaching, they're going to be bombarded with results that include the *big* coaching names, companies that train coaches, and marketers who are targeting coaches. Sure, you could spend years massaging your SEO and working your way up through the rankings, but most of the time it'll feel like you're fighting a losing battle.

Finally, this myth perpetuates another myth: that consistently posting quality content means that your ideal clients will see that content. Whether you're talking about a blog, podcast, social posts, or any other form of content, creating content is a fundamentally different task than making sure your content gets in front of your ideal clients. Yes, it's important to create content, but if it's not being seen in the first place, then it's ultimately not doing a lot for you.

This is where *finding your ideal clients becomes important*—the ability to locate exactly where your ideal clients are "hanging out" online so you can then move to the second step of the client attraction process: getting in front of them.

Your ideal clients *are* hanging out online, even if you think they aren't tech-savvy enough to be on social media. For example, with nearly 3 billion active Facebook users, it's inevitable that some version of your ideal client is there. Whether your ideal client is a busy executive, stay-at-home parent, or retired grandmother, the internet—specifically social media—is the best place to find and connect with them.

Your first job is to find them.

Much like the process of identifying your ideal client in the first place, the process of finding them depends heavily on your ability to drill down and be as specific as possible.

The best way to think of finding your ideal clients—not just online, but anywhere, for that matter—is as concentric circles.

The innermost circle represents your ideal client, comfortably situated within two larger concentric circles. This is where they "live" online; it could be their Facebook, LinkedIn, or Instagram profile, or any other very specific location where a single ideal client is and can be reached.

Fortunately, one of the things we know about humans is that we are very community-centered beings, that we gravitate towards people who are similar to us—people who share similar values, beliefs, interests, and problems. You're going to leverage this aspect of human behavior in your client attraction process because your goal, after all, isn't just to get in front of a single ideal client—it's to get in front of many ideal clients.

This takes us to the middle circle, which are the communities that your ideal clients are in. These communities can take many forms, but these are groups of people that come together around a shared interest or identity—anything from a knitting circle (interest-based) to an LGBT group (identity-based). These are groups that are centered around a commonality shared by its members. They can be informal or formal—all the way from a casual book club to a formal business networking event.

If the inner two layers are your ideal client and the communities that they're a part of, then the outermost layer is the containers that hold those communities. This could be a specific social media platform or even the yarn store that hosts the knitting circle. Throughout this process, you're going to spend the bulk of your time in the communities themselves, but it's just as important to make sure that you're spending time in the communities that are *in the right container.*

We'll talk in more depth about each of these circles in the next chapters. For now, it's important to understand the entire picture of finding your clients online, from the high-level containers that house their communities down to their individual locations within those communities.

THE OUTER CIRCLE

The outermost circle is perhaps the easiest to understand because it is by far the broadest. You know that you're looking to find where your ideal clients are hanging out online, and you know that the way to do that is to identify communities that they're a part of. To achieve that, you must start by figuring out where to look for these communities.

Since we're primarily talking about leveraging the internet to attract new clients, it really comes down to those two magic words: social media.

We'll talk in later chapters about the ins and outs of social media—stuff like posting content, engaging, and building your following—but before we talk about any of that we have to identify the platform where you're going to focus most of your energy.

It can be tempting to try to build a presence on every single social media platform there is, and there are plenty of platforms to look at—Facebook, Instagram, Twitter, LinkedIn, Snapchat, Pinterest, TikTok, Clubhouse, the list goes on. For now, especially if you're just getting started, it's best to choose one, *maybe two*, platforms to focus on. That's because you will get the best results out of your client attraction process when you dive deep into making *one* platform work for you, rather than maintaining a relatively superficial presence on many platforms.

This doesn't mean that starting on Facebook means you're tied to that platform for life, and it doesn't mean you can't expand into other platforms as you grow. It means that for now, the best course of action is to choose one platform and *do it well*.

In this chapter, we're going to look at the three most popular platforms for client attraction: Facebook, LinkedIn, and Instagram. These three platforms have a long track record of being excellent tools for attracting new clients, which is why we're going to focus our energy there. Of course, other platforms like TikTok and Clubhouse have great potential to attract new clients, but we'll not cover them extensively in this book.

When choosing a social platform as your primary client attraction tool, there are four questions you want to ask to make sure you find the perfect fit:

1. Are my ideal clients on this platform?
2. Are my ideal clients active and engaging on this platform?
3. Is there a place on this platform where groups of my ideal client are gathering?
4. Is there a way for me to directly connect with and communicate with an ideal client?

Depending on who your ideal client is, it may take some digging to find the answer to each of these questions, but if you can answer "yes" to each one of these questions when evaluating a specific platform, then it's likely a good fit for you.

Now that you have a basic understanding of what you're looking for when choosing which social media platform to work with, we're going to dive into some specifics of each of the major platforms—Facebook, LinkedIn, and Instagram—to help you make the most informed decision.

FACEBOOK

We start with Facebook because it is by far the biggest and most active social media platform in the world. With 2.89 billion monthly active users, it's a statistical inevitability that your ideal client is on Facebook.

Such a large user base is certainly an advantage because it means that you have a virtually unlimited supply of people you can get in front of, and when you focus only on getting in front of those ideal clients, you're getting in front of the *right* people. At the same time, being only one of 2.89 billion users means that it can be easy to get lost in the mix if you aren't intentional about finding communities of your ideal clients and focusing your energy there. In that sense, being active on any platform will be a *massive* waste of time if you're not dialed in on exactly which communities you're targeting. More on that in the next section.

Facebook works well with most niches, and a wide variety of life, spiritual, health, wellness, and relationship coaches have significant success using Facebook alone. This is largely due to leveraging Facebook Groups, and its broad appeal to all users combined with its dynamic groups makes it an ideal platform for finding and accessing communities filled with ideal clients.

LINKEDIN

LinkedIn is more professionally-focused than other social networks. Whereas Facebook can have a personal and intimate feel to it, LinkedIn is decidedly business oriented—which is aligned with its purpose: to promote networking and fostering connections between likeminded professionals who can support each other.

Therefore, it's a great place to find your ideal clients if you are selling to other businesses, or your ideal client's career is directly correlated to your niche and offer. If you work specifically with C-suite executives, for example, it's much easier to find and connect with them on LinkedIn than on Facebook. There are two reasons for that.

First, they are probably not engaging in the same conversations on Facebook as they are on LinkedIn. Given that LinkedIn is first a networking tool, they're likelier to conduct networking on LinkedIn and perceive Facebook as the social network for their personal life.

Second, it's much easier to filter for specifics with LinkedIn. Unlike Facebook, LinkedIn has a robust search feature built specifically for prospecting and sales. With a Sales Navigator account, you can search LinkedIn's entire user base to generate a list of prospects who perfectly fit the profile of your ideal client.

LinkedIn has approximately 30 million business professionals who have specifically joined the site to be part of a network of professional connections (as opposed to friends). The distinction between professional connections and friends is important because while your Facebook friends are likelier to engage in a friendly conversation, professional connections are likelier to engage in networking and sales conversations.

INSTAGRAM

Instagram is one of the fastest growing social networks. In 2020, for example, its user base increased by more than 145 million. Because Instagram appeals to a younger crowd, it's an ideal place to find a young adult audience as well as those who are visually oriented and appreciate aesthetics.

If you've tried marketing on Instagram before and have given up in frustration, it's probably because of one of these three reasons:

One: You weren't playing the hashtag game. Hashtags are the lifeblood of Instagram. And if you're not using them the right way, chances are slim that you're going to get your content in front of people beyond those who already follow you (more on this later).

Two: You weren't engaging with other posts using the same hashtags that you were using. Using hashtags isn't enough—it's important also to like and comment on *other people's* posts that are using the same hashtags.

Three: You weren't engaging and starting conversations. Similar to what we've already talked about in terms of the need to go find your ideal clients, if you only post content and expect ideal clients to come banging down your door, you're going to be met with bitter disappointment. It's true for all the social media platforms, but especially so for Instagram, where it's all about more genuinely connecting with your ideal clients.

I regularly see life, health, wellness, and spiritual coaches get to $10-15k/months using Instagram alone, entirely ignoring Facebook. It's all about posting high-quality content that is meticulously planned to coincide with your ideal clients' interests. It's all about starting real conversations and building authentic relationships. And it's doable.

However, Instagram is *not* for you if the thought of posting photos everyday scares you or if you're terrified of posting a selfie. Instagram's visual-oriented platform prioritizes images significantly more so than text, to the point that just posting images of quotes to your feed doesn't cut it.

THE MIDDLE CIRCLE

Once you've identified the container and platform where you want to focus, the next step is to find the communities that your ideal clients are in. One of the beautiful things about coaching is that oftentimes we (the coaches) are either a more progressed or evolved version of our own ideal client. For example, a lot of the relationship coaches I've worked with have had to work through many of the same relationship issues that they help their clients with.

Being a more progressed version of your own ideal client is a *huge* advantage because it means that when you start identifying the communities your ideal clients are in, you can start by looking at the communities that *you're already in.*

Beyond that, identifying the different communities your ideal client might be in is an excellent opportunity to think creatively about where they're hanging out. For example, say you're a leadership coach who specializes in working with professional women. Communities centered around leadership for women might be the first thing that comes to mind, but it's worth thinking through even more communities that ideal client might be part of:

- Communities geared towards professional women (not necessarily around anything to do with leadership)
- Communities of managers or executives, either exclusively women or not
- Communities centered around leadership, either exclusively women or not

You'll notice that in that example, we're looking at variations of the ideal client: professional women who need to strengthen their leadership skills. Even though your ideal client isn't a man, that's fine—there are likely going to be *plenty* of women in that community anyway. When finding communities that your ideal clients are in, you don't necessarily have to search for ones that exclusively have your ideal client. Your ideal client just has to be in there.

It's also important to remember that your ideal client exists not just in the context of your niche, but as a whole person. A professional woman who needs stronger leadership skills is not spending all of her waking hours thinking about how she's a professional woman who needs stronger leadership skills. She has other identities and interests, too, and is likely part of various communities that align with those.

This is such a key concept because you don't just want to speak to their concerns and the mistakes that they're making in terms of how you can help them, but you want to talk to them in terms that encompass the entirety of their being. If you're helping a client with their business, their business is not the only aspect of their being. If you're helping them with their health, their health is not the only aspect of their being. And the same with mindset, fitness—no matter what your niche is, it's not the only thing that they care about.

A couple of years ago I was talking with my client Anne, a body image coach who specifically helps women redefine their relationship with their bodies so that they can improve both their physical and mental health. She felt exasperated because she was having no luck finding communities of women who were having conversations about body image. In fact, she was at the point where she had convinced herself that her niche was so private and sensitive that there was no such thing as a community where her ideal clients were gathering:

> **Me:** *The problem you're helping your clients solve is poor body image, right?*
>
> **Anne:** *Yes.*
>
> **Me:** *Okay, and if you asked an ideal client what the problem is, would she say that it's their body image?*
>
> **Anne:** *No, absolutely not. She would talk about how she's too fat or too skinny or how she always feels physically exhausted or how she doesn't think she'll ever be happy with the way she looks.*
>
> **Me:** *So, they're really preoccupied with their weight, and that's a pretty recurring theme. What are they doing to solve that?*
>
> **Anne:** *They're doing everything under the sun...trying all these fad diets, juice cleanses, fasting programs. They're*

doing everything to change their weight, but nothing to improve their relationship with their bodies.

Me: *And can you find communities that have to do with these fad diets, juice cleanses, and fasting programs?*

Anne: *Oh, I've never thought of it that way.*

If you're having trouble identifying the types of communities that your ideal client is hanging out in, a good question to ask yourself is *What are they currently doing to try to solve the problem that I can help them solve?* Oftentimes the solutions that our ideal clients are trying are not at all the solutions that are going to get them sustainable results, so looking to communities centered around those solutions is often an effective way to find where your ideal clients are hanging out online.

THE TACTICS

Now that you understand the strategic piece of the middle circle—specifically, finding communities that your ideal clients are in—we can now get down to the fun stuff: where to go to find these communities.

One of the ways that you find your ideal clients online is through online communities—the places that they're already hanging out. Tactically, these look like Facebook Groups, LinkedIn Groups, and even Instagram hashtags.

Remember that when we're looking for these communities, we're not looking for communities that contain *only* your ideal clients—we're looking for communities that simply *have* your ideal clients in them. If you're a health coach who specializes in helping single moms with plantar fasciitis get in shape, you're probably not going to find an existing group or community that's quite that specific. Instead, you'd want to look at groups geared towards single moms, natural healing, and even runners.

Got it? Cool. Now let's talk about how to find these communities. The first step is to do a bit of research to identify groups and communities that contain your ideal client. Later on, we'll talk more specifically about what to do once you've identified them.

We're going to start with Facebook because it's the most popular, and because the majority of the concepts here translate directly to LinkedIn and Instagram. Even if you're not using Facebook as a part of your client attraction process, read through this section and then take a look at how these tactics translate to the other platforms.

Facebook Groups

If you're using Facebook as your primary social media platform for client attraction, Facebook Groups are the way to go. Facebook Groups are one of the platform's most popular features, with millions of different communities centered around nearly every topic.

The technical process of finding groups on Facebook is fairly simple—after all, it's one of the platform's biggest features, and they want to make it as easy as possible. It's simply a matter of searching keywords in your normal Facebook search bar (like "runners," "single moms," or "plantar fasciitis"). Once the search results populate, you can filter them to only display groups.

Finding the *right* Facebook Groups to use for your client attraction process, however, takes a little more digging. Once you identify a group that looks like it could be a good fit, there are several criteria to look for to make sure that you're looking in the right place.

First, consider the group size. Groups can vary from fewer than 100 members to well over a million. Larger groups are not inherently better or worse than smaller groups, which means that in identifying the best groups for you, it's a good idea to have a solid mix of group sizes. When making a list of potential groups, try to select one or two with larger membership sizes (10,000+ members), along with several others of varying sizes. It may be tempting to skip over the groups with only a couple of hundred members, but if it's an active group, those smaller groups are much easier to stand out in.

Next, take a look at the two most important metrics that determine whether a group is worth joining in the first place—the number of posts made in the last month and the number of new members in the past week. Your success in a group depends in large part on how active the group is. If there's little to no activity or growth happening, chances are that you're not going to have much luck there.

The number of posts in the last thirty days indicates how often people are posting, which is a clear indicator of group activity. If there have been fewer than thirty new posts in the last thirty

FINDING YOUR IDEAL CLIENTS / 103

days, it tells you that on average, the group is not active on a day-to-day basis.

The number of new members over the past seven days is important because it shows whether the group is actively growing. If several new people are joining the group each day, it tells you that the group is desirable to your ideal client; that new members are going to continue to join; and that the group is on an upward swing rather than a downward spiral.

If the group size, activity, and growth all look promising, it's time to join the group—but the process of evaluating it isn't quite over yet. Once you've been accepted into the group and can see everything that's happening inside, it's time to evaluate that activity.

Now that you can see the posts, do a quick scroll through the group feed. First, look at the *types* of posts that people are making—are they all spammy sales posts with everyone trying to sell their product or service? If so, it might be worth calling it quits and moving on to another group. Seeing a sales post here and there is not a red flag, but when a group has that overall spammy feel to it, it's likely not worth your time.

On the other hand, if the posts are mostly from people asking questions and seeking advice, or if the majority of the posts seem to be genuinely well-intentioned and spam-free, that's what you're looking for here. Activity in a group is great, but low-quality activity (spammy sales posts) and high-quality activity (genuine interaction) will dramatically impact your success in the group.

If the posts are largely high quality, there's one more thing to consider: the level of engagement that's happening on the posts. People can post in groups all day long, but the ultimate measure of a group's health is in the comments section. Throughout the client attraction process, you're going to be generating engagement and starting conversations, so the ideal group already has engagement and conversations happening.

If you're scrolling through a group's feed and seeing lots of posts but none of them has likes and comments, then it's not a very engaged group. That doesn't mean that every single post in the group needs to have 50 likes and 20 comments, but if the majority of the posts have zero likes and zero comments, it's probably time to move on.

LinkedIn Groups

If you're using LinkedIn as your primary platform for client attraction, you're in luck because the same process for Facebook Groups applies over on LinkedIn. The primary difference is that unlike Facebook, LinkedIn Groups are not as big a feature. That means that these groups tend to have lower engagement, but that doesn't mean they're not an important part of an effective client attraction process.

While you want to go through the process above and identify key groups that you can join and leverage, the way you use and engage with them will vary dramatically from how you would use Facebook Groups.

Instagram Hashtags

As you may know, Instagram does not currently have a group feature like Facebook and LinkedIn. However, the concepts we've been talking about—your ideal clients gathering in communities around a shared topic or interest—are just as relevant on this platform.

Believe it or not, hashtags on Instagram serve a nearly identical purpose as groups on Facebook and LinkedIn—to connect like-minded people and to generate activity.

The primary difference between groups and hashtags is the mechanics of how they work. While groups are a defined container that requires membership, hashtags are much more fluid and flexible, given that anyone can use any hashtag.

Much like groups, the first step is to identify which hashtags you want to pay attention to—these are the equivalent of the Facebook or LinkedIn Groups you would have identified using the process above. Rather than relying on the Instagram search bar, though, I recommend using a third-party tool such as Hashtag Slayer to identify a mix of high and low-volume hashtags. Because hashtags are so fluid, the key is to find the hashtags that your ideal clients are already using—not the ones you *think* they might be using. Therefore, I recommend using that third-party tool to search for what you think they're using so that you can identify what they're *actually* using.

Similar to groups, you want a solid mix of low and high-volume hashtags. It's much harder to get noticed in those massive

Facebook Groups, and the same applies to hashtags with 1,000,000+ posts.

As you're researching individual hashtags, pay attention to the same set of indicators to help you evaluate each one: how many posts, post frequency, types of posts, and levels of engagement. What's more, don't just look at the "top posts" that are ranking for that particular hashtag—look at the "recent posts" section as well to get a more holistic view of what people are posting with that hashtag.

THE INNERMOST CIRCLE

This brings us to the innermost circle, which represents your ideal clients' online life. Identifying the groups they're in and hashtags they're using and following is one thing, but you must also be able to *identify your ideal client when you see them*. You know who your ideal client is, but recognizing them when you see them is crucial. If you can't recognize them, you can't connect with them.

One of the greatest mentors I've had in life and business is my grandfather Jerry Hancock, co-founder of Alexander Hancock Associates, a boutique consulting agency who has worked with a number of major corporate clients over the past forty years, among them T. Rowe Price, Ally Financial, New Balance, Goodyear, and the US Navy. They're no small potatoes.

One of Papaw's (it just doesn't feel right to call him Jerry) biggest strengths that helped create such massive business and financial success was that he could recognize an ideal client damn near anywhere. One his best stories is about working at the Naval Shipyard, where he and his partner (my grandmother) Emmie were conducting a training on presentation and writing skills. While walking to lunch with the training director of the Shipyard, Papaw paid close attention to the work going on around him. He noticed that the work would be going a lot better if the managers and supervisors were communicating more effectively. So he asked the training director if he would be interested in a performance management training program.

"Hell yes," the training director said. He immediately brought Papaw in to present their program to the team of managers, who were interested in what he had to say, but didn't believe that their manufacturing processes had any significant performance issues.

Papaw pointed out the window and identified a seemingly small performance issue happening at that exact moment—an issue that added up to an annual cost of over $3 million. Papaw's training program, which would address that issue along with many others, was a mere $50,000. Chump change compared to the $3 million that *only one specific problem* was costing them annually.

Needless to say, Papaw made that sale. He was able to at $50,000 to his annual income that year, not by using any high-pressure sales tactics. It was simply because he was able to spot a problem his ideal client was having and provide a cost-effective solution.

In the context of social media, if you join a Facebook Group that at first appears to have your ideal client in it, you might start engaging in it only to realize that it does not, in fact, contain your ideal client. Or does it? Your ability to recognize your ideal clients when you see them not only allows you to better evaluate groups for your client attraction process, but also helps you determine rapidly and accurately who fits your ideal client profile—and who doesn't.

As you'll learn in the next section where we cover concrete tactics for leveraging social media, a person's social media profile stands in as a placeholder for them as a person. It's there to tell the world who they are even when they're not there to say it for themselves. However, their profile is not entirely accurate and factual, given that it is created and maintained by the person it represents. It's created by an unreliable narrator, someone who has built it with an agenda—to appear a certain way, and in all honesty, to appear in whatever way serves them the best. It's generally not a malicious practice, and it's rarely a conscious decision for someone to manipulate their online presence to fit their needs and desires. In fact, we all do it.

What that means for you, though, is that you must understand not only who your ideal client is but also how they're showing up online—because the two are seldom identical. For example, while someone may seem enthusiastic and extroverted in a Facebook Group conversation with a stranger, they may be shy and reserved, even self-conscious, in a conversation on the phone, Zoom, or in person. On the other hand, someone you see giving excellent advice online may in fact be struggling—and failing—with the exact issue they're advising on.

Who your ideal clients really are rarely translates accurately to their online presence, and that's just how it works. From looking at someone's profile, you can craft a pretty good image of who they are as a person; but oftentimes when you have a one-on-one conversation with them, they shatter that image in the first five seconds. As you begin to have more and more conversations with your ideal clients, pay attention to the trends that appear—how who they actually are aligns (or doesn't) with who they appear to be on social media.

Once you start to notice these trends specific to your ideal client, you will begin to develop the ability to take a quick glance at their profile and take an educated guess as to how much of an ideal client they are. But for now, given that you probably don't know these trends yet, it's fine to take your best guess—and to err on the side of connecting with them and finding out if they're an ideal client rather than writing them off because they don't fit your best guess.

Fortunately, though, there are many aspects of one's social media profile you can look at to evaluate whether they might be an ideal client:

- How their profile is set up (is it set up for professional networking and sales, or is it clearly meant for staying connected with friends and family?)
- When their profile photo was most recently updated (usually indicates how active they are on a platform)
- How often they're posting on their profile
- What groups they're in/hashtags they're using
- What groups they're posting and commenting in
- What kinds of comments they're leaving (advice, complaining, etc.)

These are all indicators whether someone is an ideal client, and by starting conversations with people (which we'll cover later on), you'll start to learn what those indicators actually mean in terms of your ideal client.

CONNECTING WITH YOUR IDEAL CLIENTS

ONCE YOU HAVE MANAGED to find your ideal clients online—where they're spending their time and where you can get in front of them—it's time to connect. The entire basis of my client attraction system is genuine relationship-building, so your next step is to start building those connections.

The problem with a lot of marketing approaches is that they teach you how to find your ideal clients, but don't take you much further than that. They say, "Okay, once you've found where your ideal clients are hanging out online, just put out content in front of them and BAM, the clients will start pouring in."

From my experience, and the experience of many of my clients who have tried it, I can once again confirm one thing: That's bullshit.

Nothing is going to happen in your business unless you start connecting and building relationships.

On one hand, you *could* spam the group with friend requests, and DM them your pitch immediately after. The only problem with that, is, well, several things. It's just going to piss them off. It's going to come across spammy and sleazy. Oh, and it doesn't work. If you took this approach, you could send out 1,000 messages and maybe get three or four replies—along with 997 irritated people who may or may not report you to Facebook, LinkedIn, or Instagram.

Wouldn't it be better to connect with 20 warm, interested ideal clients and get 15 responses? That's a 75% conversion rate compared to the spammer's .03% conversion rate—which might sound like too much of an increase to be real, but the difference lies in your ability to focus on quality connections and relationships over the quantity of prospects. In other words, you have to see your ideal clients as living, breathing people—not just as potential dollar signs in your bank account.

Therefore, your priority at this point is to start creating those authentic connections with your ideal clients. In this section, I'm going to teach you the key concepts you need to know to be successful: *authority, intimacy, active conversation,* and *passive conversation.* Then we're going to make those concepts come alive and take a deep dive into content creation, your social media profile, and how to begin leveraging those groups and communities that you've identified as containing your ideal client.

THE TYPES OF CONVERSATION

Before we look at the specific tactics you'll use to connect with your ideal clients, there are some key concepts you need to understand: *authority vs. intimacy* and *active vs. passive conversation*. Understanding these concepts will help you better execute the client attraction process because the better you understand them, the less you'll have to rely on this book to guide your implementation—and the more you'll be able to trust your gut.

AUTHORITY VS. INTIMACY

When we talk about how you are building relationships with prospective clients, there's an important distinction to be aware of—the distinction between *authority and intimacy*. If you've been building your business for any amount of time, you've almost certainly heard something to the effect of, "You need to build authority and show that you're *the* expert in your space." You probably know that being an authority means being the preeminent advisor in your field, and you've probably been told that showing up in that way makes the clients come crawling to you.

In using a structured client attraction process like this one, you certainly are building authority—your social media posts, engagement, and activity all build your authority. That's not the entire story, however. In focusing too much on building authority, there's ultimately nothing separating you from every other coach and consultant out there who's holding up a sign that says, "Look at me! Look what I know! Look how smart I am! I'm an expert!" Relying on your authority alone will not attract clients, and oftentimes devolves into a screaming match of "I'm more of an expert than you."

Additionally, focusing solely on authority comes at the expense of something equally (if not more) important—*intimacy*. Intimacy is the actual closeness that you create with your ideal clients— the relationships and trust that you build through that authentic connection. It doesn't have anything to do with proving that you know what you're talking about or pitching a prospect. It's all about the rapport and relationship you build with them.

In other words, intimacy is what helps you rise above the screaming match—and above all the competition trying to prove their authority—and actually gets you clients. Let's pretend there are two coaches who both help their clients with similar issues. They're equally competent coaches, and they both have a great track record of helping their clients get results. The coach who gets the client, however, isn't going to be the one who's saying, "Look at me, I'm an expert."

The coach who gets the client is the one who actually *connects* with the prospect. Maybe she made sure that her prospect really felt *heard* in their conversations, or maybe they just connected over comparing their respective grandmothers' apple pie recipes.

That's because your ideal clients don't care only about working with someone who knows their shit. They also care about working with someone they can connect with, someone they trust, and, in all honesty, someone they *like*. The same is probably also true for you—you probably only want to work with clients you actually like, too. It's a win-win.

One of the most common venues for conversations in this process is in the DMs—whether that's on Facebook, LinkedIn, or Instagram. If I were having a DM conversation from a place of establishing my authority, I'd be coming to the conversation thinking about all the advice I could give the person on the other side. I don't know about you, but personally, I really hate unsolicited advice (and your ideal client probably does, too). But if you came to that conversation from a place of creating that intimacy—or closeness—with the person on the other side, you're going to be much better received. Empathize with them, relate to them, learn about them, and above all else, build a relationship.

It's the same as meeting someone new for the first time, whether it's at a party or at your neighborhood park. You're not jumping to see how you can help them or trying to solve a specific issue in their life. And chances are that you're not thinking through each word you say, trying to figure out how you're going to get them onto a strategy session.

You're just chatting to get to know them—and that's the type of closeness you want to be creating in these online relationships.

ACTIVE VS. PASSIVE CONVERSATION

There are two types of conversation that are used in attracting new clients: *active conversation* and *passive conversation*. They are very different ways of engaging with ideal clients, and it's important to understand what they are and the role they play so that you can effectively incorporate both into your client attraction process.

Let's start with active conversation, which is more common and easier to understand. Active conversation is any direct engagement that you have with an ideal client in which there is a two-way conversation. This could be a DM conversation, a back-and-forth in the comments on a post, or a question they ask on a live webinar.

Passive conversation, however, is a bit more abstract—it's much more indirect, one-way conversation. This is when someone reads one of your social posts or watches your most recent Facebook Live. It can even be when they see you engaging in groups or on other posts.

The most important thing to understand is that when someone reads one of your social media posts and then goes about their day, *it's a form of conversation*. You just don't know when you're having it because there's no trackable and tangible engagement. Even if they don't read your post but see your name at the top of the post—that's a form of conversation.

One of the most widely accepted principles of marketing is that you must have a certain number of touchpoints between you and an ideal client before they consider working with you (some people say you need seven touchpoints, while others say you need 22; the number really doesn't matter as much as actually making those touchpoints happen). Touchpoints are those tiny instances of passive conversation, which is why they're so important.

If you're only engaging in active conversations—direct message conversations and strategy sessions—then you're going to quickly identify a bottleneck in your business, which is that you can only engage in so many of those each day. Whether it's five or fifty active conversations, there's a distinct limit to how many you can because there are only so many hours in a day.

That's where passive conversation comes into play. It prevents the bottleneck altogether. It's what allows you to get in front of infinitely more people—people with whom you've not yet had the opportunity to engage in active conversation. Whereas active conversation is much more focused and personal, passive conversation is much broader, making it ideal for warming up your ideal clients before engaging with them in active conversation.

Both types of conversation are key to an effective and *sustainable* client attraction process, and when you leverage both of them, you not only broaden your impact but also connect with more ideal clients.

CREATING GREAT CONTENT

Reading your posts is often one of the first ways an ideal client engages with you—even if they don't like or comment on it. Posting quality content is a form of passive conversation. Although it is not an effective client attraction strategy on its own, it *is* one of the cornerstones of any effective marketing process.

Content is one of those big, scary words that sends many entrepreneurs running because it can seem so overwhelming. I get it, you might feel nervous when it comes to putting yourself out there. But I'm going to break it down into the simplest terms possible and talk about what content is, what will do for you, and how to create content quickly and painlessly.

Content is really simple—it's anything that educates, entertains, or inspires. That's a pretty broad definition, intentionally so, because content can take many forms. This is fantastic because it gives you the freedom to do what works best for you.

When we're talking about how content fits into your client attraction process, the priority is to educate, the second is to inspire, and the third is to entertain (your content should be entertaining anyway, but its *purpose* is not to entertain). You'll most likely spend the bulk of your time focusing on content that educates, but you'll probably also create some content that inspires as well.

There are three reasons to create content in the context of your client attraction process. The first is to start the conversation with your ideal clients. If you start off a conversation with an ideal client by pitching them your offer, that's not going to go very well. Your prospects need to know you—or at least have some familiarity with you—before they'll ever consider working with you. In a sense, pitching your offer to a stranger is a lot like proposing marriage on the first date. Sure, it works once in a million times (I actually know of someone for whom that worked), but it's certainly not the norm.

The second reason is that your content builds authority and trust with your ideal clients, which is absolutely key. When you put out quality, relevant content to your network, you position yourself as an expert and as an authority in your space. You also begin to build trust with your ideal clients—which is so important because people aren't going to buy from you if they don't trust you.

The third reason is that content done well generates leads for you. When you follow this framework and accompany your content with a compelling call to action, your ideal clients raise their hands, saying, "Me! I need your help."

Content shows up at every stage of the client attraction process, which means it includes your social media posts, blog articles, videos, podcast episodes—any sort of communication with your ideal client is content (even your strategy sessions and DM conversations, believe it or not). And when you think of all your communications in terms of content, it's much easier to remember that what you need to be doing is educating, inspiring, and entertaining.

There are several major pitfalls that arise regarding content creation. The first is believing that you're going to be great at it from the get-go. Creating quality content that speaks directly to your ideal client is like a muscle—you have to exercise it regularly. The first piece of content you create isn't going to be earth-shattering and brilliant. And that's okay. Create mediocre content today. The next day, create slightly better mediocre content. And so on.

The second major pitfall is giving up. Saying, "Okay, I've posted content for about a week. Nothing has happened. Therefore, this isn't working." That's not going to cut it here. Creating and publishing a week's worth of content and then skipping the next week is not going to produce results, plain and simple.

It all comes down to consistency, chugging along even when writing a social post is the absolute last thing you want to do. When creating this content starts to feel boring and unsexy and pointless, it means you're on the right track because you're starting to get used to it.

The last major pitfall is trying to make your content perfect. If every piece of content you create has to be a perfect work of art, then you're not going to get anywhere. Write your piece of content, read it once to ensure it makes sense and is free from any grammatical errors, and *just post it.* Consistent imperfect action beats inconsistent perfect action ten times out of ten, and oftentimes that means hitting publish before you feel ready to put it out into the world.

CONTENT MODES

We briefly mentioned that content can come in many forms. There are three general *modes* of content that you can create: text, images, and audio/video.

Most people tend to favor one mode over another, and it's fine to pick the one that is most comfortable for you. However, you want to make sure that the mode you produce most of your content in is also the mode that your ideal client prefers to consume. How do you find that out? You experiment.

Personally, the modality I'm the most comfortable working in is text—content that communicates its meaning through writing. I am, first and foremost, a writer. And getting on camera or having my voice recorded, while far less terrifying than it used to be, is still not my preferred modality. But I knew that I had to at least stick my toes in it because when I experimented, I found that my ideal client is far likelier to watch a short video than they are to read a long post or email.

The first content modality is text—blog articles, social media posts, emails, PDF resources, and even short eBooks, worksheets, and templates. If you don't fancy yourself a writer and the idea of writing a longform social media post is terrifying, I'm sorry to inform you that while you can use as many images, audio, and video as you want, you'll never be successful without creating some written content. You're not going to be able to avoid writing social media posts, for example, but don't worry. We're going to make it as easy and as painless as possible.

The second content modality is images. To use images as content, you must have some basic understanding of design principles, even if it's just the ability to discern whether something looks "good" or "bad." But we're not just talking about cute little posts that have an inspiring quote front and center. That selfie you took last weekend while on a hike? Perfect. Add a text caption to it and post it. The bear that's digging through your trash? Post it.

Memes are a great example of image-based content. Memes can be both educational *and* entertaining, and when they're super-specific and speak directly to your ideal client, they can be an astonishingly effective addition to your social media page.

Infographics are also an option for image-based content. Infographics are straightforward images that show someone how to do something, explain a concept, share statistics, or otherwise communicate information.

Like I mentioned before, you can also create *quote blocks*, an image that features a quote, some tips and tricks, or even a testimonial. It's essentially a mashup of text and image-based content and can be a great way of making text stand out in your Facebook or Instagram feed.

The third and final type of content is audio and video, which can be ridiculously effective when done well. There are two main forms of video that you can use as content: shortform videos and longform videos.

Shortform videos range from 30 seconds to 5 minutes, and can be any combination of educating, inspiring, and entertaining. To be effective, these videos should be hyper-focused on one super-specific topic and stay 100% on topic. Longform videos, however, range from ten minutes to thirty minutes or longer. Examples of longform videos include webinars, online workshops, interviews, or video trainings.

When talking about video, one of the most common questions I hear is, "Should I go live?" If you've never done a live video before (like Facebook or Instagram Live), it may be best to upload some pre-recorded videos first, just to ease you into the process. Once you're comfortable enough to go live, I definitely recommend it. Social media platforms favor live over uploaded videos, which means that your live videos get greater visibility (and therefore more views) just by virtue of being live.

More than likely you're going to have a primary content modality that you work with, whether that's text, images, or audio and video, but for maximum visibility and success, you need to dip your toes into all three.

THE CONTENT FRAMEWORK

Now that you have a general understanding of what content is and what it looks like, we're going to focus on how to actually create content using a simple and straightforward proven framework.

Every single piece of content you create and put out into the world has two goals. The first goal remains the same, no matter what type of content you're creating: *to create a shift within your client.*

This can be a mindset shift (helping them shift their thinking) or a perspective shift (helping them realize one specific thing), but the overarching goal is to create that shift.

The second goal of your content is to prompt your ideal clients to take a specific action in light of the shift you're creating. This is known as your Call to Action (CTA), and can be to book a call with you, sign up for a webinar, opt in for a free resource, or simply to comment below with their thoughts or their answer to a question.

The call to action is important, but what dictates whether a prospective client takes that action or not isn't about the call to action itself. It's about whether they experienced the shift you're trying to create.

If you make a longform text post that creates a mindset or perspective shift in your ideal client, they'll be much likelier to act in light of that new information—which is your call to action that aligns with the post.

Similarly, if you make a longform text post that fails to create a mindset or perspective shift in your ideal client, they'll be much *less* likely to take any action—because they don't have any reason to.

That magical *shift* is the lifeblood of your content, and there's a fairly simple framework for achieving it:

Help your ideal clients realize that they're doing something wrong, show them the implications of that mistake, show them the benefit of fixing it, and tell them what they need to do to fix that mistake.

Broken down into four distinct components, your content should highlight each one of these:

- The mistake they're making
- The pain of that mistake
- The benefit of fixing that mistake
- What they need to do to fix it

Whether you realize it or not, your ideal clients are making many mistakes. Otherwise, they wouldn't have a problem. The first thing you want to do is brainstorm a list of those mistakes that your ideal clients are making—the simple and concrete mistakes:

- What are they doing on a daily basis that causes them problems?
- What *wrong* things are they doing to try to fix their problem?
- What are the things they're subconsciously doing, not even aware that they're doing them?
- What are the mundane, seemingly meaningless mistakes they're making?
- What do they *believe* about themselves or their problem that is incorrect and/or unhelpful?
- What are they doing to sabotage their own efforts for transformation?

If you're a productivity coach, you might say that your ideal clients aren't managing their time well, which directly impacts their productivity. "Not managing their time well," is a broad mistake, though, and not nearly specific enough for our purposes here. Instead of identifying that high-level mistake and moving along to the next one, dig deeper and get more specific. That's where you'll find *even more* mistakes:

- They're checking their phone throughout the workday.
- They're not prioritizing their task list.
- They're stuck in pointless meetings.
- They keep getting interrupted by their boss or coworkers.
- They don't block time in the day to get their most important work done.
- They spend the bulk of their time on the least important tasks.
- They don't plan their day ahead of time.

As you can see, "not managing their time well" is not a mistake. It's an overarching theme under which a *ton* of mistakes fit. The more specific you can get with the mistakes your ideal client is making, the more dialed in your content will be.

Once you've identified the mistakes that your ideal client is making, there are three components to identify for each one: the pain of making that mistake, the benefit of fixing it, and what they need to do to fix it.

In identifying the pain of making a mistake, consider the short- and long-term consequences that your ideal clients experience. Your ideal clients might not yet be experiencing the long-term consequences of making this specific mistake, but what happens if they continue to make it? Further, what other frustrations arise from making this mistake (that they don't even realize)? Your ideal clients might not even realize these frustrations can be fixed, but rather have resigned themselves to suffering with them.

Next, consider the benefits of fixing that mistake. If they fix this mistake, what benefits and results do they reap? Similar to the pain, continue to dig deeper and identify not just the results they experience in the weeks and months after fixing it, but in the *years to come* as well. You can take it a step further, though, and ask, once they've gotten those benefits and results, how that effects *every* area of their life.

Finally, it's time to add in the last piece of the framework: What they need to do to fix that mistake. What are the high-level actions your ideal client needs to take to solve that problem and reap those benefits? For example, if the mistake you identified is that your ideal client doesn't plan their day ahead, you might say that there are three steps to fix that: 1) At the end of the day, reflect on what they got done that day; 2) Identify what they need to do the next day; and 3) Identify when during the next day they'll complete each task.

Once you've gone through this process, you're ready to turn it into content.

Believe it or not, you're almost done—you've created something much more useful than a list of topics. You have entire outlines for juicy, high-caliber content for each mistake your ideal client is making. If you listed twenty mistakes that your ideal client is making, that means you have twenty outlines for twenty content pieces. The best part is that these are incredibly flexible outlines, meaning that you can use them for a plain old social media post *and also for a full-length blog article.* You can go live on Facebook to talk about one of these mistakes for three minutes, *or you can expand it to become a thirty-minute video training.*

Magic, right?

Let me show you a quick example, just so you can get a feel for what it looks like to turn an outline like this into a longform text post.

Here's the outline I'm working with for this example:

- Mistake: Entrepreneurs committing to many programs/ techniques/approaches that are supposedly going to help them get more clients; they're undercommitting to many different techniques.
- Pain: Wasting a lot of time and money; ultimately not seeing any progress; frustrated.
- Pleasure: Get more clients; don't resent their business anymore; more money/reach revenue goals; spending time doing what they love rather than focusing on fruitless marketing attempts.
- What They Need to Do: Identify what they actually need, find the best fit, commit fully.

With that outline in mind, here's what it could look like turned into a social post:

I've been in business for several years now, and it's not always been pretty. For the first several years, I found myself drifting...

From coaching program to coaching program...

From one guru to another...

From one magic technique to another technique...

...All trying to find the secret sauce that was going to get me the clients of my dreams.

But spoiler alert: That's not what happened. In fact, I just ended up spending over $50k just to realize one thing:

All of the $5-10k courses and coaching programs I was participating in?

I wasn't actually investing in them—I was just buying them.

I'd do "the work" that they told me to do if I wanted results...but never got those results.

And it wasn't the coaching program's fault (usually—there are some notable exceptions).

It was me—I was getting in my own way.

Not by overcommitting to too many programs and strategies, but by UNDERCOMMITTING to too many.

Would you rather:

A - Sign up for 5 programs at $10k each, give 20% of your effort to each of them?

B - Sign up for 1 program at $10k (probably less), and give 100% of your effort to it?

The answer is obvious, right? But most of us (past me included) go for Option A without even realizing it. Option A is easy—you come across a program that seems new and shiny, and you go for it. But the problem is that two weeks later, another new and shiny program presents itself.

When you choose Option B, though, you have a MASSIVELY higher chance of getting the results you want—the number of clients, monthly revenue, and extra time.

So, how do we choose Option B?

#1: Identify what it is you ACTUALLY NEED. Are you looking for a marketing program to help you get more clients? If so, where is it that you're feeling stuck? Because maybe what you need isn't marketing help at all, but rather guidance around your own mindset.

#2: Find your best fit. Once you know what it is you actually need, find a solution that feels like the best fit to you. Pay special attention to the messaging, approach, and make sure that they align with your values and beliefs.

#3: Go all in. Once you commit to a program, GO ALL IN. Give it 100%. The financial investment you make is only half of what you need to invest—the other half is your time, energy, and effort.

If someone had told me that early on, I probably would have saved $40k—and allocated that money where it would have been more useful.

So, I'll go ahead and say it: You're welcome for saving you $40k.

LEVERAGING YOUR PROFILE

Your social profile—whether that's on Facebook, LinkedIn, or Instagram—serves as your primary content hub; it's your home base that your ideal client interacts with once you've found them and have connected with them.

Did you connect with someone in a Facebook Group? They're going to click through to your profile. Comment on someone's post? Same thing. No matter what type of engagement you have on social media, all the roads lead back to your social media profile.

And that's why the first order of business here is to get that profile into shape. There are two primary components of your social profile, and each one is equally important.

The first is the *appearance* of your profile—these are the nitty-gritty things like your profile photo, cover photo, and bio, all of which need to align with your offer and brand. The second is the *content* on your profile—what you actually post to social media regularly.

OPTIMIZING YOUR PROFILE

Let's start with optimizing the appearance of your profile, which is fairly straightforward. First, it's important to note that I'm talking specifically about your *profile*—not a Facebook Business Page or LinkedIn Company Page (although an Instagram Business Profile is fine). I'm talking about using what you might refer to as your "personal profile," which might sound a bit scary at first, especially since you'll want to make your profile public after going through the optimization process below.

Yes, we're talking about using your profile, and that likely means adapting your existing personal profile for business use (*gasp!*).

There are two primary reasons for this approach:

- In 2018 Facebook made significant changes to their Business Pages, which dramatically reduced the organic reach of content posted to Business Pages. This decision was in an effort to get businesses to boost their reach by paying for Facebook Ads. Therefore, posts to a Business Page receive virtually no visibility.
- This client attraction process centralizes relationship-building, and people prefer not to build relationships with faceless businesses—they want to connect with real people. By using your own profile, you position yourself first as a human (which helps build intimacy).

So, let's optimize that profile.

First, you want to have a professional but friendly photo that resonates with your ideal client. For example, if your ideal client is a stay-at-home-parent, an austere, professional headshot isn't likely to resonate with them. On the other hand, if your ideal client is an executive-level professional, a more formal headshot is usually entirely appropriate.

The next piece of your profile is one that's often overlooked is your cover image. While Instagram does not currently have this feature, both Facebook and LinkedIn encourage you to add a cover photo to your profile. A banner of sorts, your cover photo is an ideal place to offer a quick snapshot of what you do.

I recommend a straightforward image with a one-sentence description of how you help people. Opt for a simple design that's not visually complex, and don't attempt to communicate all the details and nuances of your offer.

Then comes your profile bio, which is a brief description of what you do and who you serve. Textually, this is likely similar to your cover photo, but the main difference is that your bio should focus explicitly on the *result* that you help your clients achieve. Because there are often strict character limits on your bio length, it's important to use this space to focus on the explicit result that your ideal clients want.

One of the big questions that comes up at this point is what to do with all those old photos and posts that have been living on your profile for the past ten years. If you've been using this social profile for a long time, it's time to do a little cleanup.

First, remember that people want to work with other people, which means that *it's a bad idea to remove content from your profile that shows you're an actual person.* All of those family photos show that you're a living, breathing human like them, which helps build that intimacy we know is so important.

But the drunken college party pics? The Facebook arguments and polarizing political posts? Maybe rethink those. If it's something you don't want your ideal client to see, it's a good idea to take them down. Truthfully, you don't have to scroll through years and years' worth of posts, but go far enough back that it's unlikely anyone will see them. (Most people won't scroll through ten years' worth of old posts, so you're probably safe just culling your posts from the past year or two.)

While those key components of your profile's appearance stay fairly static—maybe getting updated every couple of months— the actual content on your profile is much more dynamic because it changes every time you make a new post.

POSTING CONTENT TO YOUR PROFILE

At this point, you're familiar with the content framework of *mistake + pain + benefit/desire + what they need to do to fix it.* This is the core template of most of the content that goes on your profile, and as we've already talked about, this can take countless different shapes—longform text posts, live video, images, etc. Roughly 50% of the posts you make to your profile should follow that formula. These posts are where you primarily offer value, demonstrate authority, and communicate who you are.

The majority of these posts should have some sort of call to action—an action that you want ideal clients to take in light of the content you presented in your post. There are a variety of types of calls to action you can use here, the most popular being to book a call with you. Because your ideal clients are at different stages in their lives or businesses, and because they are at varying levels of familiarity with you, booking a call should not be the only call to action you use in your social posts.

There are numerous additional calls to action you can use:

- Prompt your ideal clients to take an action that concretely benefits them. For example, if you're a meditation coach for people who are brand new to mindfulness and meditation, you might prompt them to take a ten-minute walk focusing on one specific aspect of their environment or self.
- Ask your ideal clients to comment below to get a free resource that will help them solve a super specific problem.
- Call on your ideal clients to click through to a piece of content that's hosted elsewhere—perhaps a YouTube video, blog article, or something else that's valuable to them.

The other 50% of your posts, however, are much more flexible. These are called engagement posts.

Engagement posts tend to be fairly short—one or two sentences at most—and the primary objective of these posts is to generate, well, engagement. It's as simple as asking a question with the intent of getting your ideal client to answer in the comments section. These posts are excellent at creating conversation, as well as helping you identify potential leads based on their responses.

What's more, it's an excellent opportunity for gathering market research.

Beware: *There is such a thing as a bad question.* Bad questions are usually leading questions, which means they're fishing for a particular answer. Bad questions are oftentimes black-and-white, with no room for nuance or discussion. A meditation coach asking, "True or False: Meditation can help manage stress" is an example of a bad question because the vast majority of people are going to respond with a resounding "Yes!" It is largely accepted that meditation helps manage stress; therefore, there's very little room for discussion beyond widespread agreement.

Good questions, in contrast, meet several criteria:

- There's no right answer—each person's response comes from their experience.
- There's room for healthy disagreement—everyone isn't mindlessly agreeing with each other.
- It causes your ideal client to pause and say, "Wow, I've never really thought of it that way before."
- It makes your ideal client feel like they have something to offer the conversation. They're not just standing on the sidelines watching.
- It makes your ideal client raise their hand and say, "That's me. I resonate with that."

Let's look at a quick example. My client John is a spiritual business coach who helps dissatisfied and unfulfilled entrepreneurs discover and pursue their unique calling—the purpose that lights them up.

He recently posted the question, "True or False: Spirituality has no role in your business." This post got over 100 responses, the bulk of which were from his ideal clients saying things like, "I've kept the two separate in the past, but now I'm thinking I need to shift my approach," and, "False. They're deeply intertwined, but I've personally struggled to align the two."

And from that question post, he booked more than ten strategy sessions with prospective clients. That's a pretty good success from just one post. But let's look at the key parts that made this question so effective:

- John phrased the question to make it about the role of spirituality in *their* business, not the role of spirituality in business in general. In doing that, John shifted the question from asking about people's opinions to asking about their lives. In doing that, he made it so there wasn't a single correct answer, and all of his ideal clients were able to offer an answer that was true for them.
- It created a perspective shift among ideal clients who had never considered that their spirituality and business were related. In asking this question, it helped them realize that it was a concept worth considering.
- It brought his ideal clients forward. On one hand, the people who said "false" were his ideal clients because they already shared a core value that aligned with his coaching offer. And on the other hand, the people who said "true" tended to be people who were now considering that connection. Both were versions of his ideal client, just at different stages of the process.

- It was a simple and short question. The question didn't come at the end of a longform text post. It was its own post, and it focused on prompting ideal clients to tell John about themselves.

Now that you know the types of posts to make, the elephant-in-the-room question that always comes up at this point is *How often should you post?* This is perhaps one of the most difficult questions to answer for someone because there are so many variables at play, including how often you can post *consistently*, what posting frequency your ideal clients respond the best to, and even what platform you're using.

But here we'll at least try to get you an answer you can work with.

If you're just getting started either posting regularly or transitioning a personal account to a business account, I recommend posting twice/day on your profile for the first week. This is called "priming" your profile, which means that much like priming a pump in a swimming pool, you're loading your profile with new content so that when your ideal clients start viewing your profile, there's already a feed of quality content they can scroll through.

After that first week—once you have ten pieces of content published on your profile—I recommend posting once each day (whether you post on weekends and holidays is your call). At the same time, once a day is merely a recommendation because consistency is significantly more important than frequency. It's better to post three times each week and do that regularly than to post three times each *day* and give up after two weeks.

Experiment with the frequency that works best for you. Just remain consistent.

Remember that your social profile is your primary content hub. Everything you do on social media ultimately leads back to your profile, which is why it's so important not only to optimize your profile to speak to your ideal client but also to post content regularly.

LEVERAGING GROUPS

For every marketing tactic that exists in the world today, there are three groups of people: the people who swear that it's the *most* effective approach to attracting clients (i.e., usually marketers); the people who swear that it's the *least* effective approach to attracting clients (i.e., usually other marketers); and the people who are listening from the sidelines trying to decide which tactic is going to work best for them (i.e., everyone else).

In reality, no one marketing tactic is inherently better than another. You have people on one side screaming "Use LinkedIn!" and people on the other side screaming "Use Facebook!" But neither platform is good nor bad when it comes to client attraction. That's because *if a marketing tactic exists in the first place, that means it's already been proven effective.*

For example, many people claim that Facebook Ads are a scam and that it's impossible to run a profitable ad campaign. That assertion is demonstrably false, given that advertisers spent $84.17 *billion* on Facebook advertisements in 2020 (compared to $69.7 billion in 2019). If Facebook Ads were not profitable for advertisers, then we would not have seen such massive 20.7% growth from 2019 to 2020.

Facebook Ads work. Facebook Organic works. LinkedIn works. Instagram works. Email works. All of these tactics work, but for them to prove profitable, they have to be *well executed.*

Several years ago, I brought Margaret on as a new client, and she was struggling to attract clients of her own. When I told her that it sounded like leveraging Facebook Groups would help her attract some great clients, her face twisted into a grimace, and she said, "I've been trying that, and it's not working." Truthfully, I already knew that she had been attempting to leverage Facebook Groups, and I already knew exactly why she wasn't getting any success from it.

First, she was trying to be active in *far too many* groups. If I remember correctly, she was trying to stay active in nearly 100 groups. She wasn't able to engage consistently because she was spreading herself much too thin. Second, when she was engaging in a group, she was making the same post in the same groups over and over again—a simple paragraph to the effect of *this is what I do, this is who I help, and please come join my Facebook Group.*

No wonder Facebook Groups weren't working for her—she was going about it in entirely the wrong way. Instead of connecting with her ideal clients, she was making it all about herself. Instead of starting conversations, she was closing the door to connection. Instead of providing value, she was asking her ideal clients to join her group—even though they had no idea who she was.

We started by whittling 100 groups down to the 20 that were the best fit. "These are your groups for now," I told her, "but pay attention to how much engagement you get in each of them and start to cull out the ones where you're not getting any traction."

Next, we looked at her content—what she was posting in these groups. Whereas she'd been posting the same generic paragraph over and over, we identified the types of content (and their objectives) that would help her get more traction—posts designed to add value and posts designed to start conversations.

Then, we discussed how she was engaging in those groups beyond posting her own content. The problem? She hadn't been doing that. Instead of connecting with her ideal clients in each online community, she was posting that bland paragraph and then moving on to the next group. It wasn't just that she wasn't responding to comments left on her own posts, but also that she wasn't interacting with any other posts or comments in the group.

So, we drew up a plan for how she was going to engage in those groups—connecting not only with people who commented on her new and improved posts, but also with other posts and conversations that were happening in each group.

Finally, we focused on how she was turning that engagement into a more profound relationship. We'll talk about that in the next section.

After working together for 12 weeks, Margaret successfully grew her Facebook Group by over 250%, and now brings in new members every day. More importantly, she is successfully leveraging her Facebook Group to book calls with prospects and convert them to paying clients. All because she was able not only to leverage Facebook Groups properly.

It's the difference between trying to put together an IKEA bookshelf without any instructions versus following the instructions provided in the box.

In this section, I'm going to show you *how* to leverage groups and communities as part of your client attraction process. Rather than just saying, "Hey, you need to use Facebook/LinkedIn Groups," I'm going to take you step-by-step through the process of using groups to attract clients.

Once you've identified the specific groups and communities you're going to leverage—whether they're Facebook Groups, LinkedIn Groups, or Instagram hashtags—it's time to start using those groups to begin building relationships with those ideal clients.

In leveraging these groups, there are two main aspects of the relationship-building process: *content* and *engagement*. While content is what you're posting in those groups, engagement is the process by which you interact and start building relationships with ideal clients. Content and engagement rely heavily on each other, which means that posting content but not engaging will not get you any results, and vice versa.

Each has an important role to play in this part of the funnel; while content serves to build authority and generate engagement, you have to follow through with engaging and connecting to build one-to-one relationships with ideal clients.

GROUP CONTENT

By now, you're probably starting to become more comfortable with content—the process of creating and posting it. In fact, all the key concepts around content that we talked about regarding your social profile remain the same here.[1]

However, there is one key difference between content you post on your profile and content you post in groups: *group content should be more engagement-focused than value or education-focused.* In the process of looking through various Facebook or LinkedIn Groups, you likely saw a lot of longform value posts that had very little engagement. While posting longform value posts may have worked five years ago, they're dramatically less effective now. People don't engage with them nearly as much, which isn't so great because you can't engage with an ideal client if your ideal clients aren't engaging with your content.

The majority of your group posts should be focused on engagement—getting your ideal clients to metaphorically raise their hands by liking or commenting on your post. We've already talked about question posts as a type of engagement post, but when we're talking about group posts, there are different *types* of question posts, each with a different purpose.

The first is a *Bomb Question*, the purpose of which is to ask a somewhat controversial question to get conversation going. If you're new to a group, this is a great way to arrive with a splash—

1: *If you're focusing on Instagram for your client attraction process, you don't have to worry about creating an additional set of content that lives in groups because all of your content lives on your profile! The concepts in this section definitely still apply, but translated for use with hashtags rather than Facebook or LinkedIn Groups.*

asking something that will raise people's hackles and spark a lively (but not toxic) conversation or debate. For example, I once asked, "Should your business be 100% separate from your personal life?" and in a matter of hours the conversation was going full force. Because the post got such great engagement, I was able to scroll through the comments, identify who among the commenters might be ideal clients, and then reply to their comments to start a more focused conversation with them.

Then, there's the *Defining Question*, which has the explicit goal of getting only your ideal clients to engage. There are a couple of ways to go about this question, the first being to directly call out your ideal client with something like, "Who here is an *x*?" It's just a simple one-sentence question, but it's a great way to get a comment thread going that enables you once again to scroll down the list of commenters and identify your ideal clients so you can respond to them.

The second way to use a defining question is a little more subtle, primarily because it speaks less to identity (i.e., who your ideal client is) and more to pain points (i.e., what your ideal client is dealing with). A really great way to come up with a defining question like this is to look back at what your ideal clients are currently doing or have tried doing to solve their pain points. For example, a meditation coach might ask, "Has anyone here tried the Calm app for improving your mindfulness? What was your experience like?" Then, as people start to respond, that meditation coach can start to engage with commenters who appear to be ideal clients. If the app didn't prove helpful to them, then they're almost certainly an ideal client for this coach; on the other hand, if the app was immensely helpful for them, it's an opportunity for the coach to ask specifically about what areas it was (and wasn't) helpful for and then determine whether they're an ideal client.

Whether you're posting a longform post or a short engagement post, remember that group posts must focus on value, engagement, and conversation, rather than sales and promotion. In fact, talking about your offer or posting a sales post in a group will usually get you kicked out. Always want to follow each group's respective rules, and even if you are in a group that allows sales posts, building authority and creating engagement always works better.

You're going to post a fair amount in groups, and there are two simple ways to gauge the effectiveness of a group post. The first is simple: The more engagement a post receives, the better the post. However, the second way digs a bit deeper into measuring the *quality* of the engagement that's happening. People sharing a variety of different perspectives and disagreeing in the comments thread tends to be quality engagement. On the other hand, when almost everyone responds in agreement that's low-quality engagement because it means that the post didn't create any perspective shifts in people or prompt your ideal clients to think of things in new ways. You want to avoid starting social media arguments by all means, but you also don't want to start a conversation that goes nowhere.

Finally, how often you should post in groups? If you're just getting started, you might have identified as many as ten or even twenty groups that contain your ideal client. That's great, but over time you're going to cull those down to the top 4-5 groups where you get the most engagement and create the biggest results.

Begin by making 3-4 group posts (total) each week. For example, for my first week I might post twice in Group A and twice in Group B. Then in the second week, I would post once in Group A, once in Group B, and twice in Group C. You can use whatever rotation works best for you, but post at least twice in one group before making the decision to continue pursuing that group or to put your energy towards other groups. You won't post in all 10 or 20 groups in one week, but slowly start to post in each of them to get a pulse on what kind of engagement you can get from each group.

GROUP ENGAGEMENT

The second activity that plays into this part of the funnel is *group engagement*, which refers to how you interact inside a group, or, in the case of Instagram, with the posts under any given hashtag.

When other group members or hashtag users post, your job is to add value and continue the conversation by commenting on those posts. It's not just limited to commenting on other posts, either. If you see a post where you don't think you can add value or strike up a conversation, look at the comments that have already been made and see if you can respond to any of those comments.

Of course, it's better not to comment on just *any* post. You want to focus specifically on posts and comments from people who appear to be ideal clients. Otherwise, you're going to spend far too much time getting into conversations with people who aren't going to work with you.

There are four primary ways that group engagement works best. The first is to *provide value by answering a question*. When a group member asks a question, whether it's for advice or how to do something specific, answer it. Boom, simple.

The second is a variation on answering the question, which is *to answer the question with a question*. Oftentimes, when someone asks a question in a group, either for advice or how to do something specific, dozens or even hundreds of other group members flock to answering that question. The result? The original poster has to sort through dozens of different opinions and is likely more confused than ever. So instead of outright answering the question, comment with a question that seeks clarification so that you can give them a better answer.

For example, if someone asked about the best online platform to host their online course, group members will likely list off their favorites—Kartra, Kajabi, Memberium, Member Vault, Memberspace, Teachable, CustomerHub, *the list goes on forever*. However, you could comment, "What kind of course content are you using—video, audio, PDFs?" or "Are you building an online community in addition, or do you just need somewhere to host the online course?" The question you ask and the answer the original poster gives helps you provide an answer that's much more tailored to their specific needs. The best part? *By getting their answer to that question, you've just engaged with an ideal client.*

The third way to engage in a group is to *provide a third option*. Many group posts tend to fixate on binary—this or that, black or white—meaning that oftentimes there is disagreement between two ideas, concepts, practices, or tools. When you spot that happening in a comment thread, you can jump into the conversation and stand out by offering a third option. This could be a compromise between the two, a way to use both, or simply an added bit of nuance. The best part is that your goal here isn't to actually solve whatever the problem is, but rather to get people thinking about things in a new way—it's the same concept as that perspective shift we've been talking about.

The fourth and final way to engage is to *preach*. Yes, to preach. Occasionally when you see a post that goes against something you believe or against something you know to be true, you have to get up on your soapbox and preach a bit. This doesn't mean that you have to be an asshole, call the original poster names, or otherwise be mean. But tell it like it is. The person you're disagreeing with likely isn't an ideal client, and will therefore never be your client, which means that you're not preaching to change their mind. *You're preaching for your ideal clients watching from the sidelines.* When you get into this sort of group engagement, pay attention to who's liking your comments. They may very well be your ideal clients.

In Facebook Groups in particular, many admins regularly make "welcome posts" asking new group members to introduce themselves to the group. These posts often garner a lot of comments from new members who are eager to introduce themselves in the comments. Keep an eye out for these posts, as these introduction comments are a great way to identify ideal clients and engage with them by replying to their introduction.

A Note on Group Rules: Most Facebook and LinkedIn Groups have their own set of rules for engagement and posts in the group.

While you always want to *follow the group rules*, it's also important to understand that in most cases the rules are your friend. The rule that forbids spam and sales posts may seem to limit what you're able to do in the group, but in reality, it encourages the exact type of authentic and relationship-building posts and engagement you're bringing to the table with this client attraction process.

Group admins create these rules to maintain the quality of any given group—to ensure that group members are not inundated with cold pitches in the comments, or worse, in their DMs. That's bad news for the coaches out there who are practicing those marketing tactics, but it's great for you because it creates the opportunity for you to stand out as someone who values and is building relationships with group members.

Regardless of what the rules are, though, it's always a good idea to befriend the group admins early on. When you have the group admins in your court, it opens the door to collaborations and connections that might not be open to most group members. For example, a couple of years ago I was engaging so much and providing so much value in one particular group that the group admin noticed and reached out to me to ask if I would consider joining as one of the group admins.

I said yes, of course, for several reasons. First, the admin badge next to my name added a level of credibility whenever I posted in that group. Second, it gave me a reason to reach out to group members. In simply asking how they were liking the group and if there was anything they'd like to see happen, I was able to start building even better relationships. Third, and perhaps most importantly, I could create both authority and intimacy by showing up as an admin (authority) while also showing up as someone who genuinely cares about group members (intimacy).

To get started, your goal should be five of these engagements each day, again cycling through the groups or hashtags you've identified as containing your ideal clients. Much like with your group posts, make sure to pay attention to the quality of engagement and responses you get to gauge the effectiveness of the group or hashtag you're using. Later on, we'll talk about how to convert that engagement into a deeper relationship.

Engagement Prompts

Finally, here are some prompts for your group and hashtag engagement—simple templates and formats to help you get started:

- There's a lot of good advice here, but really what's going to get the best results is doing these three things...
- What else have you tried to achieve *x result*?
- Love this! I've never thought about it like that before. How did you [discover *x*, figure that out, etc.]?
- Yikes, that sounds like a rough situation. I have a friend who tried *x* before—is that something you've thought about?
- I love how you pointed out *x*—have you ever thought about how that impacts *y*?

BUILDING RELATIONSHIPS WITH YOUR IDEAL CLIENTS

BY CONNECTING WITH YOUR IDEAL CLIENTS via content and group engagement, you've begun the process of planting the seeds for authentic relationships and warm, qualified prospective clients. You probably suspect that there's something more to the client attraction process, though—that there *has* to be something beyond commenting on your ideal clients' posts and regularly posting content. And you'd be correct.

In leveraging groups and hashtags, you have begun to feed the very top of your funnel. If you remember the funnel we talked about earlier, you remember that there are several steps between getting in front of your ideal clients and making a sale. This is the step in which you take those seeds you've planted and start to grow them into more substantial relationships with your ideal clients.

In this section, we are going to talk about how to turn your group and hashtag engagement into those relationships. More specifically, we're going to talk about how you start a one-on-one conversation, build initial rapport, and maybe even start to uncover some of their pain points. And then in the section that follows, we're going to cover how to turn those successful conversations into booked strategy sessions (i.e., sales calls).

Given that we are focusing our client attraction energy on social media, the primary mechanism for these conversations is going to be the platform's direct message (DM) feature. The main focus of this section is how to effectively start DM conversations with your ideal clients in a way that builds rapport and ultimately results in a booked strategy session.

THE FOUR STEPS OF DM MASTERY

One of the great failings of the entire online marketing space is the belief that when prospecting and selling online, the same rules of positive and meaningful human interaction don't apply. In other words, how your momma taught you to behave doesn't apply to social media.

This belief has viciously infected entrepreneurs everywhere. I regularly hear claims from well-meaning coaches such as, "Everything online just feels so inauthentic," and "It just feels so *sleazy*." And that's fair. There's a lot of bullshit happening online, and it gives social selling a bad rap.

In the early days of my business, I was working with businesses in the local Asheville area, attending an in-person networking events sponsored by the Asheville Area Chamber of Commerce. The first time I went to the Chamber's annual "Mega-Networking" event, I was one of the youngest people in the room. People who frequent networking events, after all, tend to be middle-aged managers and business owners, not 20-year-old ambitious online entrepreneurs.

It was the biggest and most "official" networking event I'd attended, and I paid close attention to how people were interacting, and carefully maneuvered the handshaking and conversation dynamics with nearly obsessive attention. Juggling a cup of cheap hotel coffee and a growing stack of business cards from all the people I was meeting, I handed each person one of my own cards—but I didn't start the conversation by giving them the scoop on who I was and what I did.

Instead, I focused my attention on *them* and *their business*. I made it my priority to connect with them, learn about them, and ultimately make a deeper connection than I would if the conversation had been, "Hey, here's what I do. If you or anyone you know needs me, here's my number."

As a result of that networking event, I made some fantastic connections, one of whom I still have a standing meeting with on Thursdays at 12 p.m.

When it comes to online networking or marketing, though, so many entrepreneurs throw their in-person networking skills out the window and attempt to take the quickest and cheapest route to getting clients—sometimes that's advertising, and other times it's spamming everyone they come into contact with.

As I mentioned, one of the most common sentiments I hear from my newer clients is that they feel like it's impossible to attract clients online without sacrificing their authenticity. In fact, I'll use my former client Jimmy as an example. "I just don't know how to get clients on Facebook without being spammy," he told me.

"Have you ever been to an in-person networking event?" I asked him, thinking back to my own experience.

"Yeah," he told me. "Before the pandemic I used to go to stuff like that every week, and I got so many clients out of it."

"That makes perfect sense. You connect really well with people, and when you connect with people, they want to work with you—right?"

"Yeah, it's just that online stuff that I can't do."

"Think about it this way," I began. "When you go to a networking event, you interact in a certain way, and the way you interact is what draws people to you. The same is true of showing up online to attract clients—it's the same skill set, only translated for the online space. The core principles stay the same, and the only thing that changes is the venue those interactions take place in. Instead of a hotel conference room, it's Facebook."

Jimmy looked at me for a moment, completely silent. *Oh no*, I thought to myself, *I've completely lost him*. But as I opened my mouth to explain it again, he blurted out, "Oh *man*, that's genius. I'd never thought about it that way!"

"Great," I said, "So let's talk about how to make that happen."

There are four main steps to having an effective DM conversation with an ideal client. These are mostly the same across all platforms, with some platform-specific exceptions:

1. After engaging with an ideal client, send them a friend/connection request.
2. Send an introductory message once they've accepted your request.
3. Continue the conversation and building rapport in the DMs.
4. Engage with them regularly and keep the conversation going.

If you do those four things, you'll be primed and ready to book some strategy sessions when we talk about that in the next section.

SEND A FRIEND REQUEST

This step picks up right where we left off when talking about how to leverage groups and hashtags. Once that initial engagement has happened, it's time to go ahead and send them a friend request (Facebook), connection request (LinkedIn), or give them a follow (Instagram). That initial engagement could be many things—here are some examples:

-   They replied to a comment you made on a post
-   They commented on your post
-   They liked your post

Whatever type of engagement it was, whenever *they* interact with you (such as leaving a comment), that's your signal that it's time to send them a friend request. There are several reasons we want to send them a request before messaging them directly. First, when they accept your friend request, it's actually part of the conversation—it's them nodding their head and saying, "Yes, you're someone I want to be connected with." If you skip that step and go ahead and send a message without first getting that head nod, you've set up the conversation to be one-sided. It sends the signal that you don't necessarily care if they want to be connected with you—you're going to go ahead and message them anyway. What that means, of course, is that you're not going to be as well received (if you get a response at all). Moreover, when you send someone a Facebook DM before you're friends, it gets hidden in their message requests folder, reducing the chances that they're going to see your message at all.

Second, you want to start with a friend request because it prompts your ideal client to click through and look at your profile. The previous engagement you had with that person, combined with how compelling your profile is, dictates whether your friend request is accepted. This is precisely what I meant about your profile being your content hub and that "all roads lead back to your profile." Your outgoing friend requests almost always result in profile views, which is why we spent so much time earlier optimizing it.

If their profile is public, you can increase the chances of getting them to accept your request by taking a look at their profile and commenting on one of their recent posts. This can be a basic comment, even as simple as "OMG, I love this!" Whatever comment you make doesn't even have to be related to your niche or expertise because it's more about building rapport and intimacy than anything else. When you take that extra step and comment on something on their profile, you create a touchpoint where the ideal client sees your name in another place. And as you know, those positive touchpoints accumulate to build trust and likability.

Resist the temptation to send friend/connection requests randomly to people with whom you've had no previous engagement or interaction. Sending out requests like this will result in a much lower acceptance rate, and because you've never spoken with the people you're sending a request to, they're going to be significantly less open to you starting a conversation.

SEND AN INTRODUCTORY MESSAGE

The goal of this step is simple: to start a DM conversation with an ideal client. Once an ideal client has accepted your friend or connection request, it's time to start the conversation. This may seem intimidating, but the best way to think of it is not as "starting" a conversation, but rather as *continuing the conversation that you've already begun*. Hopefully you've started implementing this client attraction process, so you've most likely already started a conversation with them in the comments in a group post, the comments of one of your posts, or even the comments of one of *their* posts.

No matter what that engagement was, it was about *something*. When we talked about profile and group engagement, we avoided cheap, meaningless comments like, "Thanks for posting!" or "This is great!" While we might have started a comment with a phrase like that, we ultimately posted comments that actually added value or asked a question. Remember, we're going for quality engagement.

Because you've been engaging on that deeper level, that engagement was the first part of the conversation, and because the engagement was about a particular topic or issue, *that's your entry point for continuing a conversation in the DMs*. Whenever writing that introductory message feels daunting, take a look back at whatever previous engagement occurred and *ground your introductory message in that engagement*.

Sending a simple DM is perhaps one of the easiest steps of the client attraction process. But it's also one of the ones where people struggle the most...*because it's easy to overthink it*. Don't overthink it, just do it. The other problem that people run into at this point is trying to talk like someone they're not—either following a script or dressing up your language to sound more professional (or in some cases, more casual). If it feels unnatural to speak a certain way via DMs, chances are that it feels unnatural on the other end as well.

What should an introductory message look like?

There are a million ways to go about it, and what your introductory messages look like will change over time as you find what works best for you. To get you started, we're going to look at a super simple formula for crafting the perfect introductory message.

The formula I recommend starting with is simple: *Statement +
Question*. Make a statement, then ask a question—you can send
these as one message or as two messages in quick succession, but
the idea is to open with a sentence that grounds this conversation
in the context of whatever previous engagement occurred, and
then to ask a follow-up question.

Let's begin by looking at some examples of statements that could
relate back to a previous engagement:

- Name! I really appreciated your insight about x, especially
  how you mentioned y! I've never thought about it that way
  before.
- Hey Name! Loved your post about x! I've started doing y
  lately, and it's really helped me to z!
- Hey Name! Love your focus on x niche. Your post on y was
  so great!
- Name! I just wanted to introduce myself, since we chatted
  briefly in the comments in the x group.
- Hey Name—I wanted to follow up because I saw your post
  on x in the y group and wanted to say that I've struggled
  with z issue in the past as well, so I totally get it.

These are just a few examples of how you could craft a statement
to open a DM conversation, but the most important thing to
understand is the strategy behind it—to begin by connecting
your initial message directly to an engagement that previously
occurred.

The second part of the formula, then, is the question. While the purpose of the statement is to open the conversation in a friendly, relatable manner, the purpose of the question is to prompt an actual conversation. When you leave the question out, you open yourself up to receiving conversation-killer replies such as "Thanks!" or worse, the thumbs up emoji. By asking a question, you elicit a higher quality response from your ideal client. And when you get that higher quality, more engaged response, you have more to work with to continue the conversation beyond there.

Obviously, your question should connect to the statement you just made (and remember that we're not waiting for a reply to the statement before sending the question; these should be sent back-to-back). Building off the statements we looked at above, here are what some of those questions could look like:

- How did you discover x?
- What made you realize x?
- Do you do x on a regular basis?
- How did you get that idea for your post?
- How did you learn x lesson?
- How've you been enjoying the x group?

This might seem a little abstract with all these *x*'s and *y*'s, so here are some examples of real-life introductory messages that have successfully been used in the past:

> *Hey Jennifer! I really loved your post about intuitive eating, especially how you mentioned that emotional eating is mostly just a default response that our bodies have, and that it's a matter of rewiring that response. How did you come to learn about that as a default response?*

> *Hey Bobby! Loved your post about being able to get in shape without having to spend hours at the gym every day. I've started doing simple 20-minute workouts lately, and I've had SO much more energy lately. Is fitness coaching what you do full time?*

> *Nate! Love your focus on working with creative entrepreneurs! Your post on making creative space in your schedule was spot on with my past experience as well. How did you find that niche?*

> *Hey Jessica! It's great connecting in the LGBT Business Owners Group :D Were you able to get your question about Kajabi answered? I saw that a lot of people replied, and I know that 100 different opinions can be overwhelming, so I wanted to make sure you ACTUALLY got your question answered.*

As you can see, some of these messages fit that statement + question formula more than others, but all of them achieve the two most important goals, which are to continue the conversation from previous engagement and to open the conversation up for a further back-and-forth.

The question that often comes up at this point is how to execute this step effectively when your ideal clients' posts and engagements aren't directly related to your niche. If you're seeing ideal clients post and engage in groups, but it's not directly correlated to the pain points you help them to solve, trying to find an entry point to engage with them can feel like grasping at straws.

If you're starting to experience this, there are two things to look at. The first is to make sure that you're in the right groups. If you're not in a group where people are actively talking about the issues that face your niche, it's a signal that you may be prospecting in the wrong place. The second is that while you ideally want to engage on posts that are related to your niche, the primary purpose of this part of the process is to get the conversation started. *So, get the conversation started.* It might feel like a waste of time to engage with an ideal client in a conversation about their grandma's apple pie recipe, but if they're an ideal client, that's still a massive win. Of course, you'll want to shift the conversation eventually, but if you're struggling to find an entry point for an introductory DM, take the pressure off to start conversations only about your niche and instead focus on getting a conversation started.

BUILD RAPPORT IN THE DMS

Once you've sent an introductory message and have gotten an initial response, your goal at this stage is to build rapport; in other words, your goal is to create a friendly relationship with your ideal clients in the DMs. You're *not* trying to book a call or pitch your offer at this point, but rather *just to get a friendly back-and-forth conversation going.*

One of the principles we're operating under in this part of the DM conversation is that people *love* to talk about themselves. The second principle is that people will only open up and reveal their true selves if they have some amount of trust in you. That level of trust varies from person to person, but it means that if you want to get your ideal clients to open up to you, they have to like and trust you. That brings us to the third principle, which is the best way to build trust and to get others to be vulnerable is to be vulnerable yourself. Remember in the previous section when we looked at a statement that said, "I've struggled with *x* issue in the past as well?" That's a perfect example of what we're talking about here. Now, that doesn't mean that you should spill the beans and tell your entire life story, but it does mean that sharing intimate tidbits about your life and your past can be a really effective way to build that trust.

In addition to being vulnerable as a way of creating the space for your ideal clients to be vulnerable, the other key practice here is asking good questions. Remember that one of our goals here is to get a friendly conversation going and when they have some amount of trust in the person they're speaking with, people *love* to talk about themselves. And asking the right questions can get that ball rolling.

Asking questions as a way to create that back-and-forth is an incredibly effective tactic for building trust. However, there are two pitfalls that it's essential to avoid. First, make sure not to turn your conversation into an interrogation. Asking questions is great, but your ideal clients will start to disappear if they start to feel like they're in an interrogation room. The best way to avoid that is to actually *respond to their answer*, rather than just barrel ahead to the next question. A simple, "Yeah, I've had a similar experience," or "That's nuts, I've never heard of something like that happening," can go a long way in terms of making the conversation more authentic. You probably do this in your daily conversations anyway, so do it here as well.

The second pitfall to avoid is giving unsolicited advice. Most people don't take too kindly to it, and it's also just kind of rude. At the same time, you *do* want to provide value, which means it's important to understand that value and advice are two different things.

For example, a really effective way to provide value rather than giving advice in the form of "You should do *x*" is to frame it as a question: *One of my friends tried x, and it really helped him to y. Is that something you've thought about?* While the former comes across as a bit arrogant and perhaps even presumptuous, the latter is a more conversational approach that creates value in a friendlier manner.

Regarding what questions to ask during this stage of the DM conversation, *the best questions are those that flow naturally with the conversation.* That may seem like a vague answer, but if you're having a natural conversation, then it's genuinely impossible to follow a set of scripted questions.

However, *the next best questions help highlight your ideal client's challenges and pains.* These questions are directly related to your niche, and more specifically, directly related to the issues you help your clients overcome. Further, these questions serve as an effective way to begin transitioning the conversation into the context of your niche if it has drifted to another topic.

Questions asked at this stage (or really any stage) should not be leading questions, which means that it's poor practice and ineffective to ask questions that are fishing for a specific response (that is one of those sleazy sales tactics we don't care for). Instead, these questions should be open-ended and even perhaps a bit vague to allow for a bit of interpretation.

For example, here are some questions a wellness coach might ask:

- What are you doing to take care of your mind and body?
- How've your energy levels been lately?
- What are you doing to relax?
- How is your work affecting your health?
- What daily mindfulness practices are you doing?

As you can see, we're not digging into more in-depth questions like, "What have you tried before?" or "Is living a healthier lifestyle a priority for you right now?" Instead, we're keeping it light and friendly, while also gathering some information on their current situation.

No matter how many questions you ask or how much value you provide, your primary goal here is simply to get that back-and-forth engaged conversation going. Not focusing on booking a call or pitching your offer. Just a conversation. And then in the following sections we'll talk more explicitly about how to turn these conversations into booked calls—but first, there's one more small step to cover.

ENGAGE & KEEP THE CONVERSATION GOING

DM conversations are dramatically different from most other types of conversations. Whereas a phone call or in person conversation has a clearer beginning ("hello") and end ("goodbye"), a DM conversation starts with hello, might be followed with a short back-and-forth conversation, and then usually falls off when one person doesn't reply. That doesn't happen on the phone or in person—rarely will you say something and the other person either doesn't respond or simply hangs up/walks away. It's rude on the phone and in person, and whether you think it's rude for that to occur in a DM conversation, it happens. A lot.

Therefore, it's important first to know that *when the other person does not respond, it rarely means that the conversation is over.* They could have been messaging you from the waiting room at the mechanic, or simply had to set their phone aside to get back to work. Whatever the reason, DM conversations are inherently more ephemeral by virtue of them largely occurring on mobile devices in between trying to do other things (working, taking care of kids, grocery shopping, mowing the lawn). Unlike you, who is using DMs as a prospecting tool, your ideal clients are not sitting down specifically to have a DM conversation with you.

It can seem frustrating at first, but it's actually part of what makes DMs so effective. Because they're a series of short exchanges that take place over a span of time to form one larger, more complete conversation, it means you have more leeway to follow up and reignite the conversation.

Your DM conversations will naturally fall off, and rather than letting that be the end of the conversation and dismissing them as a prospective client, your goal at this point is to stay engaged with them and continue the conversation. There are two ways to do this: engaging with them and direct messaging them.

The first is fairly simple—engaging on their profile from time to time. I recommend maintaining a list of ideal clients with whom you want to stay connected and make a habit of commenting on one of their posts at least once a week. This can be a simple "Love this!" or "Gorgeous photo," but the idea is to keep yourself at the top of their mind.

The second is to follow up directly in the DMs. Obviously, you want to avoid messaging them every day and harass them, but a simple check-in can be really effective. For example, "Happy Friday! How's your week been?" is a great way to reignite a conversation. Alternatively, you can follow a similar approach to what we discussed in Step 3 and follow the statement + question formula to continue the conversation.

Doing those two things is an effective way to continue building relationships with your ideal clients, and the next step is to turn those conversations into booked strategy sessions.

BOOKING CALLS WITH YOUR IDEAL CLIENTS

ONCE YOU'VE ESTABLISHED A CONVERSATION with an ideal client, it's time to take the next step in building the relationship: Set up a time to chat with them.

This entire process depends on two key concepts.

Concept #1: *The best way to sell your coaching or consulting program is to get on a call with your prospect,* whether that's an old-fashioned phone call or a Zoom call. You've probably heard lots of promises and strategies for selling your coaching without getting on a call with your prospect. Save your time and money because if you're a new coach, those strategies won't work for you. Those tactics are only effective for established coaches who already have a steady stream of new clients. They're great for taking on more clients and scaling your business, but less great if you don't already have a healthy lead flow. Therefore, the best way for you to sell your coaching program is to *get on a call with your prospects.*

Concept #2: *If you don't ask your prospect to get on a call with you, they're not going to get on a call with you.* It may seem simple, but it's one of the biggest issues I see with new coaches—you have a healthy list of prospective clients, but you're not booking any calls because you're not asking for the calls. It's easy to think that a social media post with your booking link will suffice, but the best way to book calls is to be direct and personal—send your prospect a message and ask if they'd like to get on a call with you.

There was a period in my own business when I was feeling especially beat down by my business, when I was busting my ass day in and day out on social media, making some great connections and having lovely conversations, but not booking any calls. In all honesty, it was pretty depressing. I was pouring so much time and energy into connecting with my ideal clients online, but I was having almost no strategy sessions.

I was starting to feel burnt out. I was having so few strategy sessions, I wasn't making nearly as many sales as I wanted, and I was slowly becoming demoralized.

Then I had an epiphany. And it was kind of embarrassing, honestly. Once I saw it, I wanted to smack my palm into my forehead, it was that damn obvious:

Out of the hundreds of qualified prospects I had great conversations with over the past several months, I had asked almost none of them for a strategy session.

You won't book the call if you don't ask for the call.

These instances of asking for the call are *Set Attempts*. A set attempt is the act of reaching out to a prospective client and *attempting* to *set* an appointment. Set attempts are one of your most important metrics to pay attention to because the more set attempts you make, the more strategy sessions you book, and the more strategy sessions you book, the more sales you'll make.

There's this myth out there that if you create a booking link so that anyone can get on your calendar with just a few clicks, all you have to do is put it on your website and social media. Suddenly, your ideal clients are going to start booking time with you—and all you had to do was put that booking link out into the world.

Yes, you should still do that, but *no*, you should not rely on that to book calls with prospective clients. Doing that may result in a few booked strategy sessions, but it's generally the exception to the rule that *you have to ask for the call.*

You can try it for yourself. Go post your booking link on your website and social media and see how many qualified strategy sessions you book that week. Then come back and implement the tactics in this section and see how many qualified strategy sessions you book for yourself...just by directly asking for the call.

THE TWO TYPES OF CALLS

Before we can dive into set attempts, we're going to briefly cover the two *types* of calls that you're going to be booking in this process: *Triage Calls and Strategy Sessions*. You're likely familiar with the idea of a strategy session, but perhaps less so with its little brother, the triage call. We'll talk more about how to conduct each of these calls when we tackle the sales conversation, but for now, it's important to understand the differences between them.

First is the *Triage Call*, which is also often referred to as a "quick consult" or "connection call." It's usually 15-20 minutes long, and it serves to build rapport, determine whether the prospect is an ideal client, and book a strategy session if they are indeed a solid prospect. Because this call is centered around rapport-building and information-gathering, it is the best option when you're not certain whether a prospect is an ideal client. There is never a pitch at the end of this call. Instead, if you think they are a good fit, you give them the opportunity to talk further with you about what working together would look like.

The second type is the *Strategy Session*, which is frequently called a "free consultation" or a "discovery session." This is more of a formal sales call, usually 30-45 minutes long, and is reserved for prospects who show all the characteristics of an ideal client—meaning you've interacted with them and gathered enough information to feel strongly that they are a good candidate for your program. The purpose of this call is to dig deeper into the prospect's pain points, help them identify what's holding them back, and share your offer with them if you're confident that you can help them.

In building relationships with your prospects, you're going to be booking both these types of calls, so it's important to understand when to use each one. As we continue in this section, we'll look at the different scenarios in which it makes sense to book a triage call or a full-on strategy session.

MAKING SET ATTEMPTS

Now that you have a working knowledge of the two types of calls that you'll be booking, it's time to dive into the different types of set attempts, which call it makes the most sense to book, and how to implement each one.

TYPES OF SET ATTEMPTS

The first type of set attempt is the *Cold Set Attempt*, which is when you offer a call to a prospect who doesn't know you and whom you don't know either. In this type of attempt, you're taking an uninformed guess whether they're an ideal client. As a result, this set attempt type has a comically low success rate. If you've been annoyed with getting cold pitches in your DMs, then you're intimately familiar with this approach. Don't do this. It doesn't work, and annoys people, making them less likely to connect or become clients.

The second type of set attempt is the *Warm Lead Set Attempt*. This means that you've been building rapport with a prospect and then transition the conversation into asking for a call. You'll have a much higher success rate. First, because you've gotten to know them, you already know they have a problem you can help solve. Secondly, because you've built enough rapport that you're confident in making the ask, they are much more likely to say yes.

This should be the set attempt type you use the most. Whether you use this type to book a triage call or strategy session depends on the level of rapport you've built and the information you've gathered. If you've managed to build a bit of rapport but aren't quite sure whether they're an ideal client, then the best route is to attempt to book a triage call. Here are two examples of what that language could look like:

> *Hey Mandi! I am super-turbo-loving the energy you're bringing to your business, so I wanted to reach out and see if you'd like to connect sometime next week for a quick call to see how we might be able to support each other.*

> *Hey John! Been a while since we chatted, so I wanted to see if you'd have time to connect next week to learn a bit more about what you're doing and explore ways we might be able to support each other.*

As you can see, the language here is fairly soft and doesn't allude to there being an upcoming pitch or an offer on the table—because there isn't. Remember that a triage call *never* ends with a pitch or an offer—that's reserved for the strategy session. In fact, if you're super-turbo-worried about this set attempt being misconstrued as an attempt to get on a sales call, you can even end the message with something like, "I promise I've got nothing to pitch ya," or "Not a sales call, promise." If you do choose to include that promise in your set attempt, then be doubly and triply sure not to pitch your prospect during this conversation.

On the other hand, if you've built a bit more rapport and have had enough of a conversation to know that they're almost certainly an ideal client, the best route is to try booking a strategy session. Keep in mind that it's a larger time commitment for your prospect—which means that it's important to be clear that they're going to get value out of it in return for taking the time to speak with you. And because it's a larger time commitment for you as well, make sure that you have a good idea that they're indeed an ideal client. Here are a couple of of how to approach this:

> *Hey Mark! I've really been enjoying the client success stories that you've been posting! I wanted to check in to see if attracting more clients is a priority for you. If so, I'd love to set up a time to chat and learn a bit more about your business and see if we can pick apart what you could be doing to make that happen. Is that something you'd be interested in?*

> *Hey Kevin! I've been loving your content—your post about your physical fitness journey was super inspiring. I really appreciated how you highlighted that you don't have to spend hours in the gym every day to be fit and healthy. I wanted to send you a quick message to see if attracting more clients is a priority for you right now. Because if so, I'd love to set up a time to chat to learn a bit more about your business and see if I can help. AND if it's not, I'd still love to set up a time to chat bc I'm really loving your stuff and would love to connect either way :)[1]*

---

[1]: *Notice that these two examples aren't identical—it's not a process of crafting one really good set attempt message and copy/pasting it to send to everyone, but rather a really personalized message geared towards each specific person.*

When setting a strategy session, the language is more explicitly sales-oriented and clearly defines the purpose of the call—to learn about them and their situation, then to see if you can help. That's because you don't want to spend 30 minutes on a strategy session and then at the end catch your prospect by surprise when you share your offer with them. When you're clear that the objective of the call is to see whether they're a good fit for your program, you ultimately book strategy sessions with higher quality prospects who are much likelier to end up working with you.

The last type of set attempt is the *Hot Lead Set Attempt*, which is by far the easiest type of set attempt because it requires the least effort on your part—that's because it's when someone explicitly says (either in the DMs or elsewhere) that they are interested in learning more about what you do and whether you can help them. In this case, it's simple: Get them on your calendar.

However, remember that you want to book strategy sessions only with ideal clients. Therefore, you have two options when you receive a hot inbound lead who wants to talk with you. The first is simply to book a triage call with them, responding with something like, "Sounds great! Why don't we set up a quick 15-minute connection call to get to know each other? Then, if it's a good fit, we can chat about what it would look like to work together." The advantage of taking this approach rather than jumping to booking a 30-45 minute strategy session is that you have the opportunity to make sure that they're an ideal client before committing to a longer conversation.

The second option is to ask a few more qualifying questions in the DMs before booking a strategy session. This allows you to gather some of the same information that you would normally get during a triage call, just in the DMs. The only significant downside to this approach is that because it takes place in the DMs, it's more difficult to get an accurate read on the prospect's personality—sometimes you just have to talk with someone to see if the vibe is right. However, if you're not spotting any red flags in your DM conversation, this can be quite an effective way to skip the triage call altogether and go straight for the strategy session.

When using this second option, you can respond with something simple and to the point like, "Thanks so much, I'd love to chat! What exactly are you interested in working on in your life (or business, mindfulness, health, etc.)?" It's a simple question, and the purpose is to make sure that they understand what you do and that they're not looking for a weight loss coach when what you really do is body image coaching. Then, depending on their answer, you can respond with a follow-up question that helps qualify them, perhaps something like, "I can definitely help with that. How long have you been dealing with that?" or alternatively, "What have you tried in the past?" It's best to only ask a few of these qualifying questions, but once you have a pretty good idea that they're an ideal client, you're all set to book a strategy session with them.

WHEN TO MAKE A SET ATTEMPT

Now that you understand the mechanics of a set attempt—the primary scenarios you'll encounter and how to handle each one—

the next question is *when you should make the set attempt*. How much rapport is enough rapport? How long should you wait? How do you know when it's appropriate?

Fortunately, this part is perhaps the simplest to answer. *As long as you've established some amount of rapport with a prospect, they're fair game to attempt to book a call with.* The amount of rapport you've built and the level to which you think they're an ideal client both dictate whether you book a triage call or strategy session, but either way, they're fair game.

When we talked about DM conversations, one of the things we highlighted was that these conversations are ephemeral and non-linear, which means that they naturally fall off and pick back up. As humans who are most used to linear conversations with a concrete beginning ("hello") and end ("goodbye"), it can be tempting to think of these DM conversations in the same way—thinking that once a DM conversation drops off, your opportunity to book a call with that prospect has disappeared, and that if you want to book a call with them in the future, you have to start an entirely different conversation with them and rebuild that rapport before you can make the set attempt. Luckily, that's not the case. Because DM conversations are ephemeral and non-linear, you don't have to limit your set attempts to new connections with whom the conversation hasn't (yet) fallen off. Anyone with whom you've previously built rapport is a candidate for a set attempt, which means that the longer you implement this daily client attraction process, the larger your pool of prospects for booking calls grows.

USING THE POWER HOUR STRATEGY TO BOOK CALLS

You now know what set attempts are, how to successfully make them, and when it's appropriate to make one. Now I'm going to teach you the concrete, repeatable process for consistently booking calls.

The best way to book calls regularly is by implementing the Power Hour, which is a 60-90 minute session when your sole focus is reaching out to schedule calls with prospects. Simple. 60-90 minutes of focusing entirely on set attempts.

Very few of the DM conversations you have will immediately result in a booked triage call or strategy session, but that doesn't mean that your rapport-building effort was all for naught. In fact, these situations lend themselves perfectly to the Power Hour Strategy because many of these will be prime candidates for a set attempt.

Before we jump into the process for implementing a Power Hour, there are three important concepts that will boost your success. The is to always prioritize warm connections over cold ones. Because the whole point is to book calls with prospective clients, it stands to reason that you're going to book the most calls when you focus on prospects with whom you've established good rapport.

The second is that when revisiting previous conversations with the intent of booking a call, you do *not* have to go back to square one and rebuild any rapport that you've previously established. That pre-existing rapport does not magically disappear once an initial conversation falls off, and unless it's been years since you've last talked with someone, you don't have to start from scratch.

That takes us directly to the third concept, which is that the most effective way to book calls during a Power Hour is to be direct about each set attempt and avoid small talk where possible. Don't start by drumming up a small talk conversation. Make the set attempt in the first and only message that you send them. We've looked at a couple of examples previously, but here's another one for your reference:

> *Hey Mark! I've really been enjoying the client success stories that you've been posting! I wanted to check in to see if attracting more clients is a priority for you. If so, I'd love to set up a time to chat and learn a bit more about your business and see if we can pick apart what you could be doing to make that happen. Is that something you'd be interested in?*

IMPLEMENTING THE POWER HOUR STRATEGY

The actions you take during these 60-90 minutes are simple. You're just sending DMs. The level of success you experience with a Power Hour depends on your ability to curate a list of prospects and focus all of your attention on booking calls—and following this routine helps you do just that.

The Power Hour has three simple steps:

1. Set a target number of booked calls and set attempts
2. Build a list of prospects you want to book a call with
3. Make a set attempt with each prospect on your list

Set Your Targets

Before getting started, there are three goals to identify—the number of calls you want to book, the number of set attempts you are going to make, and how long you're going to spend making those set attempts.

First, identify how many calls you want to book as a result of this Power Hour. Remember that the number of strategy sessions you conduct is directly correlated with how many sales you make, so if you know that you can turn 20% of strategy sessions into a sale,[2] then you need to conduct five to make one sale. When you're just getting started, aiming for five strategy sessions/week is a good place to begin.

Once you know how many strategy sessions you want to book,

2: *If you don't know what your close rate is (i.e., you don't yet have enough data), 20% is a conservative average that you can begin with.*

identify how many set attempts you need to hit that target (i.e., successful set attempts); not every set attempt results in a booked strategy session, which is why we treat these as two separate metrics. How successful your set attempts are depends on a variety of factors, including the level of rapport you've built with a prospect, how intensely a prospect needs their problem solved, how willing they are to act, etc. Therefore, your set attempt success rate varies based on who you're asking (more on that in a minute). For now, it's safe to assume a 20% conversion rate from a set attempt to booked strategy session—which means that one in five set attempts will result in a strategy session.

If you want to book five strategy sessions, you must make 25 set attempts.

The third and final number to decide on is how long you're going to take to implement this Power Hour—how long you're going to dedicate your attention and focus to these set attempts. Power Hours generally run 60-90 minutes, but if this concept is new to you, then I recommend starting small with 60 minutes and increasing your Power Hour duration as you build stamina. The reason you identify a preset time limit is to keep you hyper-focused on a specific task for a finite amount of time, which helps you complete the task in a shorter amount of time than if you were to just put it on your to-do list and get around to it when you get around to it.

This means a distraction-free zone. Turn off your phone. Turn off your computer notifications. Find a quiet space. Eliminate all distractions. During a Power Hour, you have an ultra-specific task and there is no room for scrolling mindlessly through

Facebook or responding to any texts. If you've struggled with this type of focus in the past, there are some great apps on the marketplace that eliminate all distractions from your computer and even block your computer from accessing websites apart from those you need to get your work done (hint: the only website you need to be on during a Power Hour is Facebook, LinkedIn, or Instagram—whichever one you're primarily using to attract clients).

Build Your Power Hour List

This simple tactic will make the difference between a wildly successful Power Hour and a legitimately awful one: *Identify who you're going to attempt to book a call with* before *sitting down for your Power Hour.* This is your Power Hour List.

When you build your list of set attempts before you get started with your Power Hour, you're significantly more efficient. You're able to "get your head in the game" and knock each set attempt out one right after the other rather than make one set attempt, figure out who the next prospect is, and then make another. This builds momentum and puts you in a state of flow, wherein every second of the Power Hour is spent taking massive forward-moving action and no second is wasted.

Moral of the Story: Build your Power Hour List *before* your Power Hour.

With that in mind, let's talk about how to actually build that list. The length of your Power Hour List should reflect the number of set attempts you're going to make, so if you're going to make 25 set attempts, it needs to have at least 25 prospects on it. However, it's not a bad idea to pad it a bit so that you have some room to make changes if you find that someone on the list isn't someone you want to attempt to book a call with after all.

The big question is *how to build your Power Hour List*—where to source the names so that you can fill it with the warmest, most ideal prospects in your network. Because the Power Hour works best when you prioritize the warmest relationships, the best source is your previous DM conversations—either conversations that have fallen off or that have hit a lull. The reason we look here is that these are the prospects with whom you've already built some level of rapport, and likely have an idea of whether they're an ideal client. Plus, if you're regularly adding new friends/connections and are starting conversations with them (which you should be doing), that's the perfect place to look. Scroll through your DMs and identify the people you've previously talked with whom you want to book a call with. (Hint: you can mark these conversations as unread so that they're easier to find when you go back to make a set attempt with them).

Beyond that, there are several other helpful places to source prospects for your Power Hour List:

- Previous triage calls you've had with people who weren't a good fit at the time
- People who previously indicated interest in working with you but for whatever reason did not end up booking a strategy session
- People who you've engaged with in the comments to the point that you feel like you've established a fair amount of

rapport without having a DM conversation

- People on your email list (if you have one) with whom you've not had a direct one-on-one conversation in a while
- Past clients who are no longer working with you, but who might be a good fit for your recently revamped offer

Execute the Power Hour

Once you know the metrics you're trying to achieve and have a strong Power Hour List that will help you achieve them, it's time to sit down and implement your first Power Hour. Remember to set aside all distractions, and once you've done that, the rest is dead simple. Set your timer for 60 or 90 minutes, sit down at your computer, and follow this simple process for each person on your Power Hour List:

1. Pull up that person's conversation in your DMs
2. Write a personalized set attempt message
3. Hit send
4. Repeat

Sound simple? That's because it is. It is perhaps the simplest process to effectively book calls with your prospects, and the only requirements for it to be successful are a) a strong Power Hour List of warm leads, and b) the focus to sit down and message each of them.

Once you complete your first Power Hour, you'll have a better idea of how often you'll need to implement the Power Hour Strategy to consistently book calls. For example, if after performing several

Power Hours you know that you can sit down for 60 minutes and book five strategy sessions, and you only need five strategy sessions each week, then you can do just one Power Hour each week. On the other hand, if you need fifteen strategy sessions each week, then you would do three Power Hours.

CLOSING SALES WITH YOUR IDEAL CLIENTS

A COUPLE OF YEARS AGO I was on a call with a guy named Chris, a sales rep for one of the most prestigious coaching companies in the United States, and he was trying to sell me a $10k coaching program to help me grow my business.

It was a great program—something I knew could be a game-changer for my business—and I was pretty certain that I was going to chunk down the $10k to work with that company.

"Alright," he said as the call was wrapping up, "I can take your credit card number whenever you're ready."

"No, I'm not quite ready," was my response. "I need to think about it."

Chris went silent for a moment and then said, "I thought you were committed to making this happen."

"I am," I said, "I just want to think about it before I make such a significant investment."

"I don't understand," he said. "It sounds like you're not really committed if you're not ready to get started. What are you scared of?" I could hear the frustration in his voice, and it was clear that this wasn't going as he had anticipated.

We were at an impasse: He wanted my credit card number, so he could close the sale. And I wasn't going to give it to him. Not without taking a few days to think about it.

"I'm not willing to move forward without thinking about it a bit more," I said. "But here's what we can do: I'm happy to set up a time in a couple of days to check in."

"We can definitely do that," he said, without skipping a beat. "If you want to schedule a follow-up, we do ask for a completely refundable $1,000 deposit to book that follow-up call."

"I'm not doing that."

"I think you're just scared," he said. "I think you're scared of doing something that would transform your life and your business."

Silence. Silence on both ends.

"I'm sorry, Chris," I said. "But it's not going to work out."

I hung up.

Just writing about this interaction, even though it happened over a year ago, makes my blood boil. But I'm doing it because there is one important lesson to be learned: You don't have to be a jerk to get clients.

When we think of sales, many of us have a certain image that comes to mind—often a balding guy who's pushing his wares on you, doing everything possible to make a sale. He's throwing in extras and bonuses, trying to convince you that this is the best deal you're going to get anywhere, that in fact he's *losing* money on this deal (a lie). The phrase "used car salesman" gets thrown around a lot to describe this type of person. On top of all that is the salesman's level of confidence; never have you seen someone so confident that this particular 1995 Toyota Corolla is *the* car for you. Oh, and it's always a he—because somehow sales is reserved for the aggressive, pushy white man who doesn't like to be told "no."

If that's the kind of scenario that pops into your head when you think of sales, it's no wonder you think that selling your coaching or consulting program seems icky. That type of sales *is* icky, and it's not reserved for the used car lot, either. So many coaches these days use sleazy, slimy sales tactics not because they're sleazy and slimy themselves—but because that's what they're being taught by *their* coaches. One of the most recurring comments I hear from my new clients is, "I don't know how to sell my offer without being *that guy*." And we all know who "that guy" is—it's the used car salesman we just talked about.

The good news is that *it's your business*. You don't have a money-hungry boss looking over your shoulder and chastising you for not squeezing every last penny out of each person who walks through the door. Because it's your business, you have the agency to sell in a way that *feels good to you* and *works*.

The purpose of this section is to give you the tools to create a sales process that aligns with you, not to give you a generic sales call script and send you on your merry way. Sure, I can give you the words and phrases that have been proven to work, but if they're not *your* words and phrases, they don't work. It doesn't feel natural to you.

When talking with a prospective client, the more natural and relaxed you approach the conversation, the better results you'll experience. The person on the other end of the call *always* picks up on the energy that you're putting out, and what you receive in return is often a reflection of how you're showing up to the call. Therefore, one of the biggest things we're going to cover in this section is the mindset required for a successful sales call.

The second piece that we're going to talk about is the structure of a call; instead of handing over a script, I'm going to show you the components of a successful sales call and how to piece them together in a way that works for you. Then, we're going to talk about the part of the sales conversation that can seem the most intimidating: objections—how to ethically respond and work through your prospects' concerns before purchase. Finally, we're going to focus on follow up and nurture—how to maintain relationships with ideal clients who are not yet ready to buy.

To get started, though, we're going to take a look at the two types of calls you'll be conducting as part of your sales process: the *Triage Call* and the *Strategy Session*.

THE TRIAGE CALL

The Triage Call is often referred to as a "quick consult" or "connection call." It's usually 15-20 minutes long. The purpose is to build rapport, determine whether the prospect is an ideal client, and book a strategy session if they are. Because this call is centered around rapport-building and information-gathering, it is ideal for situations when you're not certain if a prospect is an ideal client. There is never a pitch at the end of this call. Instead, you offer the opportunity for them to talk further with you about working together.

There are four parts to an effective Triage Call, each of which builds off of each other to make booking a full strategy session together the natural next step:

1. Re-Establish Rapport
2. Set the Agenda
3. Gather Information
4. Transition the Focus

In this chapter, we're going to look at each of these four parts in detail so that you can effectively leverage triage calls to book more strategy sessions.

Step 1: Re-Establish Rapport

By the time you are on the phone with a prospective client, you have likely built some amount of rapport with them, usually through a DM conversation. Therefore, the call starts with a friendly and familiar tone as you re-establish the rapport. You can do this in just 45-60 seconds.

The easiest way to do this is to open with a comment that relates directly back to the previous interaction you've had, using that conversation to establish this new one. For example, if you previously had a DM conversation with Fred who mentioned that he's moving to Bali to build his online coaching business, you might open with, "You mentioned that you've just moved to Bali, right? How was that move for you?" The goal here, much like any new interaction, is to get a back-and-forth conversation going so that you can dive into the meat of the conversation having established a friendly dynamic.

However, be careful how much time you spend on this part—this should be 45-60 seconds at most. This is a single quick exchange to establish the tone of the conversation. Spending too much time on this comes at the expense of covering less ground in the remaining time allotted for the conversation.

Step 2: Set the Agenda

Once you've had that quick exchange to set the tone, your next step is to communicate the agenda of the call, establish yourself as the leader, and prepare them for the rest of the call. There are four main points to communicate during this part:

1. Emphasize that you're working in a set timeframe.
2. Clarify the issue at hand.
3. Help them understand the reason for the questions you'll be asking.
4. Promise to hook them up with a relevant and actionable piece of advice or content to help them solve the issue at hand.

Here's an example of what that could look like:

> **Coach:** *We only have 15 minutes together for this call, and I have a call right after this one, so is it cool if we go ahead and get started?*
>
> **Prospect:** *Sounds good*
>
> **Coach:** *Perfect, so just to make sure I understand, you're seeking clarity on how to do x, is that right?*
>
> **Prospect:** *Yeah, that's the big thing right now for me.*
>
> **Coach:** *Got it. What I'm going to do if it's okay with you is ask you a few questions just to make sure I get the full picture, then after that I'll see if I can give you some clarity on how to do x. Is that okay?*
>
> **Prospect:** *Yeah, of course.*

As you can see, it's a straightforward part of the triage call, wherein the main focus is to clarify expectations for how the rest of the call is going to go. Like the previous part of the triage call, this one should also take no more than 60 seconds, but

204 / CLIENT ATTRACTOR

that doesn't mean it isn't necessary. Skipping this part can lead to misunderstanding and awkward situations during the call, whereas including it often leads to the prospect opening up a bit more and being more honest (since they understand *why* you're asking them questions and that their honesty is directly tied to the quality of advice they'll get from you).

Step 3: Gather Information

The purpose of this third part of the conversation is to ask your prospect questions that do three things—identify the pain they're in, clarify their desire, and see what solutions they've tried before. Digging deeper into their pain, desire, and solutions enables you to better understand the full scope of the problem at hand, which allows you to better serve them during the fourth and final part of the call.

The information-gathering phase should last around 8-10 minutes, and throughout this process, be mindful of how much *you're* talking compared to how much *they're* talking. While your role is to ask relevant and helpful questions, theirs is to answer those questions and expand upon their answers as much as they want. Therefore, you should be talking 10% of this time, and the prospect should be talking 90%.

As far as what questions to ask, these questions can easily be divided up into the three objectives—pain, desire, and solutions.

Pain Questions

As we've mentioned, the objectives of the information-gathering stage are to a) understand the full context of the problem (i.e., the pain) at hand, and b) understand how that problem is affecting them. When you do this, you also help your prospect better understand the problem, which often results in new realizations and ideas on their part.

Here are some examples of pain-related questions:

- Is there a specific part of x problem where you're feeling stuck?
- Where exactly are you feeling stuck?
- How long have you been dealing with x issue?
- How is x issue affecting other areas of your life/business?
- How are you currently dealing with x issue?

As you ask pain-related questions, avoid just running down a list of questions. Instead, dig deeper into the prospect's responses with probing questions. Taking this approach helps you get to the root of the problem while prompting your prospect to think more deeply about the problem than they might have in the past:

- What do you mean by that?
- You mentioned y. Can you tell me more about that?
- Why do you think that is?

Desire Questions

Once you have a better understanding of your prospect's problem, the next step is to find clarity around the desire—the outcome they want and how achieving that outcome will change their life or business. Again, this is not only about you better understanding their current situation, but also about the gaining more in-depth clarity on their desired outcome.

Here are some examples of desire-related questions:

- What goal are you trying to achieve by solving x problem?
- How would solving x problem affect your life/business?
- If you solved x problem, what would that allow you to do in your life/business?
- How would solving x problem change how your life looks 10 years from now?

Solutions Questions

The final objective of the information-gathering stage is to understand why they're still struggling with this problem. Why haven't they managed to fix it yet? Have they tried other solutions in the past? Or have they just not tried to solve it in the past? And if they haven't tried to solve it yet, why are they trying to solve it now? This final objective is crucial to creating a smooth transition into the fourth and final stage of the triage call. Having a clear understanding of what they've tried in the past will ensure that you can provide the highest value for them and ensure that you're presenting a new solution.

Here are some examples of solutions-related questions:

- What have you tried in the past to solve x problem?
- What limitations or drawbacks have you encountered in trying y solution to solve x problem?
- Are these limitations something you'd like to fix so that you're not relying on y solution to solve x problem?
- With your current approach to solving x problem, how confident are you that you're going to solve it?

Step 4: Transition the Focus

Once you've completed the information-gathering stage and have a solid understanding of your prospect's pain, desire, and solutions, it's time to move on to the final stage of the triage call. The purpose of this stage is to give some genuine feedback and actionable advice, and then attempt to book a strategy session with them.

There are several strategic pieces to incorporate at this stage. Including them all will ensure a smooth transition from questioning to advice and from advice to booking a strategy session.

The first is to *provide relevant, actionable, and specific advice*. This can be in the form of spoken advice, but it can just as easily be a video training or resource that you promise to send them as soon as you get off the call. While this advice should be focused on the problem at hand, it should also be fairly high-level—three to four actionable steps are perfect for this scenario.

The second is to *qualify the advice you've just given* by addressing the fact that this one thing (piece of advice, training, exercise, etc.) isn't going to solve the problem in its entirety. Let them know it will get them going in the right direction, but the problem they're dealing with is fairly complex and sophisticated. This helps your prospect understand that solving the entire problem is a longer process that requires deeper guidance and coaching.

The third part of this stage is to *end the call by booking a strategy session*. This is as simple as letting your prospect know that you're out of time for today and offering a second conversation to dive deeper. Because you've just emphasized the complexity and sophistication of the issue they're dealing with, they are aware that you've only touched the tip of the iceberg in this conversation; therefore, they'll be much more likely to take you up on the offer.

However, if you get to this last part of the triage call and are fairly certain that this person is not an ideal client, there's no rule that you have to offer them a strategy session. In fact, the whole point of a triage call is to offer strategy sessions only to the people who are ideal clients. In this case, you can simply end the call after giving them a piece of advice, thanking them for their time, and letting them know that they can reach out to you if they have any questions. Alternatively, you can point them to another coach or consultant if you know someone who may be better able to them.

Finally, a common concern that arises in this final stage of the triage call is, "What if I don't come up with actionable advice to give my prospect?" If you're the type of person who needs time to absorb what's been said before responding, the idea of offering insight or advice on the spot might seem intimidating.

Rest assured, as you conduct more calls, you'll begin to notice recurring themes—the most common situations your prospects are in, and the bite-sized advice that goes with it. The more triage calls you have, the easier it will become to offer valuable insights on the spot.

If you're still feeling anxious about blanking when it's time to offer advice, there is one quick tactic you can lean on. Remember your list of specific problems that your ideal client is facing and the mistakes that they are making? If you have clearly defined your ideal client, and the prospect in question is indeed an ideal client, then chances are that you have already identified at least part of their situation when you compiled that list. And on that list, you also identified what your ideal client needs to do to solve that problem—that's the actionable advice you can give them. All you have to do is give the advice you've already written out, simply tailoring it a bit to the prospect's unique situation.

THE STRATEGY SESSION

The second type of call in the sales process is the *Strategy Session*, which are often called a "free consultation" or a "discovery call." This is a more formal sales call, usually 30-45 minutes long. It is reserved for prospects who you have a good idea are an ideal client. This call isn't offered until you have enough information to make an educated guess that they are a good fit for your program. The purpose of this call is to dig deeper into the prospect's pain points, help them identify what's holding them back, and share your offer with them if you're confident that you can help them.

In this chapter, we're going to start by looking at some important principles to keep in mind when conducting a strategy session. Then, we're going to look at the structure of a strategy session, how each piece fits together, and how to have a successful call.

STRATEGY SESSION PRINCIPLES

Before we dive into the structure and flow of the strategy session, there are some key sales principles to touch on. While the structure of the call is more logistical and revolves around what to do and when, these principles are more mindset-oriented. Understanding and embracing them will help you conduct better strategy sessions:

1. The strategy session is not solely about making a sale. It's about helping your prospect better understand the problem at hand, so they can make an informed and empowered decision.
2. Show up as an expert advisor who diagnoses the problem and provides a solution.
3. Only pitch to people who *want* to be pitched to. Otherwise, you're wasting your breath.
4. Listen to your prospect and make them feel heard. They need to trust that you fully understand their unique situation.
5. Stay on topic and don't jump to giving advice. This is a conversation about solving the problem, not a conversation that solves the problem.
6. You're leading the conversation, not them.
7. It's okay if they turn out not to be a good fit. Point them in the right direction anyway.

Principle 1: Enable Empowered Decisions

Oftentimes, we pay attention to only one metric of whether a sales conversation is successful: Did it result in a sale? That's a horrible way to look at it. If your close rate is at a respectable 20%, that means you're going to view 80% of your sales calls as failures. That's a quick path to demoralization and burnout. Nobody can keep going when they feel like they're failing 80% of the time.

What's more, treating a sale as the primary metric for success completely fails to consider many other factors that are entirely beyond your control:

- Whether the prospect is a good fit in the first place
- If they can afford to work with you
- Whether the timing is right for them
- If you even *like* each other

The good news, though, is that the primary purpose of a strategy session isn't to make a sale. It's about *helping your prospect better understand their problem and situation, so they can make an empowered decision.* Most of the time when a prospect gets on a call with you, they don't fully understand their situation, even if they think they do. It's not their fault. It may be the result of blind spots (we all have them) or merely a lack of information. That's why coaches play such an important role. It's your job to identify and dig into those blind spots, then provide them with the information they need to fully understand their situation.

A successful strategy session is one that results in an "aha" moment or realization for the prospect. The sales piece only comes in as an option to act *in light of that new realization.*

Principle 2: You're an Expert Advisor

Imagine walking into a doctor's office and barely sitting in the seat before she hands you a prescription for some drug you've never heard of. "Excuse me," you might say, "but I haven't even told you what's wrong." Has that ever happened to you? No, probably not, because that would be gross malpractice on the physician's part.

The more common scenario is that the physician asks you what's going on, maybe digs a bit deeper into understanding some specific symptoms, and then gives you a diagnosis. She then prescribes a solution, sometimes in the form of a drug, other times in the form of lifestyle changes in diet and exercise. If the physician is really excellent, she'll also explain her *reasoning* for prescribing a solution. This increases your trust in her advice because it shows that she thoroughly understands the problem, making you much more likely to follow her recommendations.

In the context of a strategy session, *you're the physician.* Your role is to understand and diagnose the problem, then prescribe a solution. In fact, you're an excellent *physician* who explains the reasoning and thought process behind your prescription.

When you approach a strategy session with this mindset, you position yourself as an expert advisor—the equivalent of a physician in your own space. The result is that you build trust with your prospect by demonstrating to them that you have their best interest at heart—not your own.

Principle 3: Don't Pitch to Everyone

While you want to reserve your strategy sessions for people who fit your ideal client profile, you won't know if they're ideal until you've spoken with them in-depth. There are a variety of reasons that the prospect on the other end of a strategy session might not be a good fit. Sometimes you'll encounter ideal clients who seem perfect...except for the fact that they're not interested in working with a coach or a consultant at the moment.

It's going to happen, and that's fine. There's a simple principle to help make every strategy session avoid awkward situations and go more smoothly: *Only pitch to prospects who want to hear your pitch.* That means only sharing your offer when you think it's a good fit, and **they want to hear about your offer.**

Your warmest prospects will outright ask you how they can work with you. This is an ideal situation, wherein you've had such a successful conversation that they're eager to hear how they can work with you. Most of your prospects probably won't ask to hear your pitch, but you can easily find out if they are open to it. It just takes a simple ask—something like, "I can definitely help you with x problem. Would you like me to tell you about what it would look like to work together?"

When you pitch only to people who want to hear it, the whole process feels smoother because you've gotten their go-ahead instead of blindsiding them with your offer. Otherwise, the pitch can feel stilted and awkward, zapping your confidence and making them much less likely to say yes.

Principle 4: Listen & Make Your Prospect Feel Heard

Throughout the strategy session, you ask your prospect a series of questions to help fully understand their situation. But what often gets overlooked is how to listen to their responses and make them feel heard. When your prospect feels like you are really hearing what they have to say, it creates confidence that you actually understand the problem and situation they're facing.

Everyone thinks that their specific situation is 100% unique to them. As an expert in your niche, you will likely see the same situations over and over again, just with minor varying details.

But for your prospect, it *is* unique to them. It's important that, even though you've seen this prospect's situation a million times, *they still need to feel that you understand them as an individual.*

Use active listening techniques like repeating back what they've told you or leading into your response with, "In light of what you said about *x*..." This communicates to your prospect that you are both listening and understanding what they've said. And if something comes up that you don't understand, don't hesitate to ask a clarifying question. Asking a follow-up question isn't a reflection of your ability to understand your prospect. Instead, it's a signal that you're not only hearing what they're saying, but you're also listening and trying to understand.

Principle 5: Remember the Purpose of the Conversation

The purpose of the strategy session is to better understand your prospect's situation, desires, roadblocks, and to offer them a solution. During this conversation, it can be easy to slip into giving your client advice or even coaching them like you would if they were already your client. You want to avoid that, not because you want to avoid giving away too much information but because actively trying to help your prospect solve their problem during a strategy session comes at the expense of better understanding their situation.

Whereas during a normal coaching or consulting call you would guide them through the process of solving their problem, that's not the goal of a strategy session. The strategy session is inherently different because it's a conversation about solving the problem—*it's not a conversation that is meant to solve the problem.*

For example, on a strategy call, your prospect might say, "I'm having trouble sleeping and I think it's because of my anxiety." It might be tempting to abandon the structure of the strategy session and jump straight into helping them immediately solve the problem—perhaps by suggesting a specific meditation or giving them strategies to cope with their anxiety so they can sleep better at night.

Instead, the better course of action is to continue digging into your prospect's problem—ask about their sleep habits, anxiety triggers, and how it's affecting their daily life—so that you can better understand their situation.

It's often tempting to turn your strategy session into a coaching call and start solving their problem. If you do this, you're missing a vital opportunity to gather more information that may lead to the root of their issue. By staying curious and getting a complete picture of their situation, you'll be better able to provide higher quality solutions later on.

Principle 6: You're in the Driver's Seat

One of the first things you'll notice when we talk about the structure of a strategy session is that in the first few minutes of the call, you are going to set the agenda for the meeting. One of the reasons we do that is to establish leadership, to demonstrate that you are the one leading this call, not the prospect. A strategy session is only effective when you are the one steering the conversation. If you don't assume that position, the prospect will notice it and do the only natural thing to do in that position—*they* assume leadership of the conversation.

You're not micromanaging the conversation, but you are setting the terms of "this is what we're talking about right now," and "this is what we are going to talk about next."

Occasionally, you will experience a strategy session with someone who refuses to let you take leadership of the conversation, either because they have their own internal need to be in control, or they have a more assertive, controlling personality. Because the strategy session is in large part the process of *you* interviewing *them* to see if you want to work with them in the first place, you'll need to decide whether this aspect of their personality would hinder the coaching or consulting process if you were to take them on as a client. Chances are that if conducting a strategy session with them is painful, working with them as a client will be, too.

Principle 7: It's Okay if They're Not a Good Fit

We've already alluded to this principle, but it's so important that it warrants talking about specifically. There are many people you'll speak with who turn out not to be a good fit, for a variety of reasons as to why that's the case. And that's okay.

If they're not a good fit, do not enroll them in your program. Don't even pitch to them. Only take clients whom you know you can help.

But what do you do when they're not a good fit?

As we've discussed, one of the top priorities of the strategy session is to help your prospect find clarity on what they need to do to solve their problem. If you're not the person who can help them do that, you probably know someone who is.

One of the most powerful things you can do towards the end of a strategy session with a prospect who's not an ideal client is simply to be honest. "Look, I'll be honest with you," you might say. "It sounds like you're dealing with x, and my expertise is really around y. I don't think I'm the person who can help get you where you need to be, but do you have a pen and paper handy? Because I want to give you the name and contact info for someone who might be able to help."

If you're an impact-driven coach or consultant who wakes up every morning excited to make a difference in your clients' lives, then that is the type of integrity to display when you're on a call with a less-than-ideal client.

But what if they're not an ideal client...*yet*? This happens just as often: You speak with someone who *could* be an ideal client, but who needs to make some more progress or understand some key concepts before they're a perfect fit for your program. In that case, identify the most immediate work they need to do to get to that point and gift them one of your free trainings or resources that will help them do that. Then, promise to follow up with them in a few months to chat about their progress. Again, do this by simply being honest, telling them, "Hey, I think you could be a great fit for my program, but you need to work on y issue before I can really help you get results." Again, *that's* the type of integrity that'll help you grow your business.

STRATEGY SESSION STRUCTURE

Now that you understand the seven primary principles of an effective strategy session—and an effective sales mindset as a whole—we can now take a deep dive into the flow and structure of a strategy session. In the previous chapter we alluded to different pieces of this conversation. In this one we are going to take a look at the structure as a whole and then examine each component in much greater detail.

The strategy session contains eight consecutive steps, each one serving a very specific purpose in the conversation. When well-executed, these steps combine to fulfill the larger purpose of the strategy session itself—to understand your prospect's situation and present a solution.

The first step is to *Open & Set the Agenda*, which gets the call started and set expectations about how it is going to go. The second step is to *Understand Why They're Here*; the purpose is to identify what your prospect wants out of the call and why they scheduled it in the first place. Once you have that high-level understanding of their needs, it's time to transition to the third step, which is to *Understand Their Situation*. In this step, you dive more deeply into where they are now and ask questions to get the full picture of their current situation.

With that more nuanced understanding of their situation, you're able to progress to the fourth step, which is to *Unpack Their Pain*. During this part of the conversation, you explore how their situation affects them in the different areas of their life and business by asking focused questions. On the flip side, you also want to *Identify Their Desires*, the fifth step, during which you uncover what they really want in their life or business, and again, how achieving that would impact every aspect of their life or business.

Now that both you and the prospect have the *entire* picture, it's time to get real and ask the hard questions to *Create Responsibility*. You've identified their goals and desires, so in this stage you must find out what's stopped them from achieving them, and then to help them take the responsibility required to achieve them.

This takes us to the penultimate step, which is to *Highlight the Gap*, the purpose of which is to summarize the entire conversation thus far and show them what's missing between where they are now and where they want to be.

Then, and only then, can you move to the eighth and final step, which is to *Share Your Offer*. If they're interested in working together, it's time for you to share your killer program and enroll them!

And boom. You've made a sale.

If the whole process seems overwhelming, don't worry—we're going to break down each step for you so you can understand each part.

Step 1: Open & Set the Agenda

When opening a strategy session, there are three primary steps that make a massive difference in how the call will go. First, open the conversation by establishing some light rapport—just spending a few seconds opening the conversation with a friendly tone. The second is to establish the purpose of the call, which is as simple as clarifying that they are here because they're interested in solving a particular problem or making progress toward their goal. The third is to set the agenda for the call, explaining briefly how the call will go. This process is quick and should generally take no more than three or four minutes. That doesn't mean these three or four minutes aren't important, though, because they dictate how the rest of the conversation will go:

- It establishes a relationship between you and the prospect.
- It ensures that you're both on the same page concerning the purpose of the call.
- It establishes leadership, communicating that you are the expert conducting this call.
- It sets up expectations for what the call is going to look like.

Here's an example of what this part of the strategy session could look like:

Coach: *Hey, is this Joe? It's Jacob Ratliff, how's your week going?*

Prospect: *Hey! It's going pretty well. How about yours?*

Coach: *It's going great! Remind me, where in the world are you based?*

Prospect: *I'm over in Seattle, how about you?*

Coach: *That's right, I thought you were somewhere in the Pacific Northwest. I'm over in Asheville, NC—known for our craft beer and hiking.*

Prospect: *Ah, yeah, I've heard a lot of great things about Asheville; never made it out there, though.*

Coach: *Definitely worth a trip if you're ever out this way. Well, let's go ahead and get started if that's cool with you.*

Prospect: *Yeah, definitely.*

Coach: *Great, so I understand that you're interested in getting some clarity around attracting more clients, is that right?*

Prospect: *Yeah, I've tried several different things and some of them have worked, but I've not found anything that works consistently.*

Coach: *Yep, for sure. I hear that all the time. Let me explain how today's call will go and then we can get started. I'm going to start by asking you some questions about your business and see if we can get you some clarity on that. And then, if it sounds like I can help and if it feels like a good fit, I'll explain what it would look like to work together. Sound good?*

Prospect: *Yeah, sounds good to me.*

As you can see, the language I use is informal and friendly. At this point it's all about establishing the tone of the call and easing any worries that the prospect may have about finding themself on a high-pressure sales call.

Once you've gotten the call started and laid out the agenda for your prospect, you can move on to the next step of the strategy session.

Step 2: Understand Why They're Here

This is when you begin to transition into the "meat" of the call—the part where you dive into their current situation and how it's affecting them. In the previous step, you clarified the overarching purpose of the call; in the example I showed you, that purpose was to help the prospect gain some clarity around attracting more clients. In this part of the strategy session, though, you're going to dig a bit deeper to better understand their motivation for being on the call in the first place.

When you fully understand your prospect's motivation, you begin to see the layer of the situation that's below the surface—why it's an issue they want to solve rather than something they are willing to live with.

Again, this is a fairly quick step, and I recommend going two levels deep after the initial question. What I mean by that is to ask the initial question, and then, based on their answer, ask a follow-up question to get more detail, and then to do the same thing one more time based on their second answer.

The initial question you ask at this stage should be fairly simple and straightforward. This could be something like, "What motivated you to take the time out of your day to have a call with me?" Alternatively, you could ask, "What would you like to get out of this call today?"

More important than the initial question, though, are the follow-up questions; while your prospect's answer to the initial question may communicate their high-level motivation for scheduling a call with you, it's usually just the tip of the iceberg. Therefore, your next step is to dig a little deeper with a couple of follow-up questions to see what's under the surface:

- *What do you mean by x?*
- *You mentioned x. Can you tell me more about that?*
- *How long have you been dealing with x?*

These are fairly simple questions, and you'll notice that there are a variety of different ways that a prospect could answer them. The reason we use somewhat general questions at this point is to allow the prospect to communicate anything that's coming to the surface for them. They may not even answer the question you asked, but the way they answer gives you a glimpse into their underlying motivation.

Step 3: Understand Their Situation

Now that you have a better idea of what's motivating your prospect, it's time to get an even deeper understanding of their situation. Being thorough in this stage is what allows you to be effective in the next step of the conversation, wherein you'll be uncovering the pain they're experiencing as a *result* of their situation. That's why it's *essential* not to get ahead of the process. This step is all about getting clarity for both you and your prospect your prospect about *where they currently are*, not how it's affecting their life or business. In even simpler terms, your objective here is to identify your prospect's baseline.

This step consists primarily of asking relevant questions and digging into your prospect's responses; remember that the goal is not to give them advice during this step, but rather to ask clarifying questions.

Before diving into asking these questions, it's important to *transition* into this part of the call. When you set the agenda, you let your prospect know what to expect. In that same vein, a transition at this point should a) let your prospect know where they are in relation to that agenda, and b) communicate *why* you're asking questions that might feel a bit personal or even intrusive.

There are a variety of ways to make this transition, but it should be no more than two sentences wherein you summarize their motivation and tell them why you're going to ask some more questions. An example of this language could be, "Sounds like you're dealing with *x*. Let me ask you a few questions to see if we can pick apart what's happening here." It's that simple.

Now you can begin the process of asking questions to better understand their current situation. These questions are more niche-specific, meaning that the questions a business coach would ask would be very different from the questions a fitness coach asks, and those questions would be very different from the questions a spiritual coach asks.

With that in mind, I'm going to outline several sets of questions that relate to different niches. Even if your niche isn't represented here, these examples will nonetheless show the *types* of questions to ask at this stage.

Notice that each of the questions below is neutral, and they avoid getting into the weeds about the prospect's pain points; instead, they aim to identify the context in which the pain is taking place (you'll dig into that pain in the next step).

Business Coach

- How long have you been in business?
- What kinds of clients do you work with? What do you help them achieve?
- How are you pricing that?
- What problem are people facing that motivates them to work with you?

Fitness Coach

- How old are you?
- What health issues, if any, do you currently have?
- How much physical activity do you get on a daily basis?
- What does your diet look like?

Spiritual Coach

- What spiritual or religious background, if any, did you grow up with?
- How would you define spirituality?
- What's the role of spirituality in your life?
- Do you have a daily spiritual practice? If so, what is it?

Step 4: Unpack Their Pain

Once you have a better understanding of your prospect's current situation, move to Step 4, where you examine their circumstances more critically. The purpose is for you and the prospect to get an even clearer perspective of how it's affecting them. In other words, this is where you *work with the prospect to help them identify their pain points.*

Structurally, this step is identical to the previous one, but the difference lies in the purpose of each question. Although they are very similar, these steps must be done separately because to truly understand your prospect's problem, you first need to see the backdrop against which it's taking place. Now that you've seen that backdrop, it's time to explore what's creating their pain.

Like the last step, the questions you ask here are niche-specific, so I'll once again give examples for a business, fitness, and spiritual coach. These questions should tie back directly to the context-based questions in the previous step and should also be adapted to reflect your prospect's responses.

Business Coach

- What is your current process for getting new clients?
- What limitations or drawbacks have you experienced with that process?
- Are these limitations something you'd like to fix so that you're not relying on x process?
- With your current strategy/approach, how many new clients are you bringing on each month?

Fitness Coach

- What are you currently doing to take care of your physical body?
- Where are you feeling stuck when it comes to taking care of your health?
- What's the biggest thing that's holding you back?
- What's stopped you from overcoming x?

Spiritual Coach

- How is not having a consistent spiritual practice affecting you and/or your relationships?
- What are your go-to coping mechanisms when you're feeling x?
- Do you think those coping mechanisms are healthy or unhealthy?
- What are the long-term consequences of y coping mechanisms whenever you feel x?

Step 5: Identify Their Desires

Congratulations! You have successfully uncovered your prospect's motivation, situation, and pain points. The most successful and ethical sales strategies *do not rely on fear as the primary motivator*, which is why the next step is to focus on your prospect's goals and dreams. Instead of scaring your prospect into believing that they're going to have an apocalyptic future if they don't work with you, you're going to *get your prospect excited about the possibilities that the future holds*. In addition, you're going to help them envision how their life or business will be dramatically different if they take action to create their desired changes.

This step consists of asking 2-3 questions that are fairly niche-specific, but are largely formulaic. The first question should ask your prospect to pinpoint a concrete, time-based goal. In the previous step, you helped your prospect identify what they *don't* want, and this question is designed to help them identify what they *do* want. By adding a time-based element to it (i.e., six or twelve months from now), however, you help your prospect begin to see the goal in more realistic terms—helping them to realize that their big goal might be more quickly attainable than they originally thought.

The second question helps your prospect to think more deeply about their goal, so that they envision how achieving that goal would impact their life or business. Oftentimes, when we think of the goals we want to reach, we identify the goal and then don't think much more deeply about it. We might still pursue the goal and take actions that we think will help us get there. But when we don't understand how that outcome affects our lives or businesses, we run the risk of not having the motivation required to keep going until it's done. Therefore, it's important to help your prospect understand the massive impact of achieving that goal.

The third question is somewhat optional, but I recommend using it because it helps your prospect expand upon how achieving their desire would impact their life or business. Whereas the second question is concerned with how achieving x result would impact one area of their life, the third question digs deeper and asks how achieving x result would affect *other* areas of their life. Oftentimes, when we ask a prospect how something will impact their life, the prospect responds with the most obvious area of impact.

For example, someone who wants to lose 20 pounds might say that losing that weight would make them feel better physically and have more energy. While that's true, losing 20 pounds probably also has other impacts beyond having more energy— perhaps it's the physical stamina to be able to play in the yard with their young child, or even just to feel sexy in the mirror.

When we think about how achieving our goals will affect our lives, it's easy to jump to the most obvious answer; but when we go a layer deeper and examine how it will impact *all* areas of our lives, we begin to think of it less as a simple goal and more as an entire transformation. Suddenly, it's about much more than losing 20 pounds.

As I mentioned, these 2-3 questions are fairly niche-specific, but still formulaic. With that in mind, I'm going to use the same examples of a business, fitness, and spiritual coach to show you what this looks like in practice.

Business Coach

- You mentioned that you're bringing in x (number of clients or amount of revenue) each month. Six months from now many/much (clients or revenue) do you want to bring in each month?
- How would bringing in x (clients or revenue) impact your business?

- How would getting to x (clients or revenue) impact other areas of your life?

Fitness Coach

- Where do you want your health to be 12 months from now?
- How would achieving that impact your life?
- How would achieving that impact other areas of your life?

Spiritual Coach

- Compared to where you are now, what would spiritual alignment look like for you 12 months from now?
- How would becoming more spiritually aligned impact your life?
- How would achieving that impact other areas of your life?

Step 6: Create Responsibility

After helping your prospect identify a more concrete goal and see how achieving that would transform their life, your objective is to help them take responsibility for their future. It's tie to challenge them and to help them be honest with themselves about how committed they are to making a change.

We do this because in order for someone to invest in transformation—whatever that transformation may be—they must understand what's preventing them from achieving that change on their own. It's also important to get them to emphasize to themselves the importance of the goal and to be realistic about their level of commitment.

This part of the strategy session does exactly that through these three simple questions:

1. You're currently at x *(current situation)*, and you want to be at y *(desired result)*. What do you think is stopping you from achieving that on your own?
2. On a scale of 1-10, how important is that goal to you?
3. On a scale of 1-10, how *committed* are you to making that happen?

Your prospect's answers to these questions are a critical part of the sales conversation. In many ways they are the final qualifying questions to ensure that your prospect is not only an ideal client, but also an ideal client *ready to do the work required to achieve their goal*. If you work through these questions and find that your prospect isn't entirely committed to their goal, chances are that they're not going to say yes if you share your offer with them.

Step 7: Highlight the Gap

It is crucial that you nail these first six steps. If you have, your prospect has a much deeper clarity about what's stopping them from achieving their goal on their own, how important their goal is to them, and a renewed commitment to achieving it. Your next step is to highlight the gap between where they are now and where they want to be. This is a perfect transition to sharing your offer with them, and also primes them for the pitch.

The first part of this stage is to recap your prospect's vision and obstacles. This can be as simple as, "Just to make sure I have this right, you'd like to achieve x, y, and z, which would mean that you can a, b, and c. But the biggest thing that's standing in your way is q."

The purpose of recapping your prospect's vision and obstacles is to show them the gap between where they are and where they want to be—which highlights that *it's going to be much more difficult for them to keep trying to do it alone.*

There are a variety of ways to phrase this, but your recap should include these three core elements:

- The goal that they identified earlier in the conversation
- How achieving that goal will impact their life/business, and how it will affect other areas of their life/business as well
- What's stopping them from achieving that goal on their own

After offering that recap, confirm that you've got it right (i.e., "Does that pretty much summarize it?"), and then let them know that this is definitely something you can help them with.

Then, ask the one simple question that's going to transition you to the pitch:

Would you like to know how we can work together?

There are, of course, some alternative ways to ask that last question:

- Would you like to talk about what it would look like to work together on that?
- Is this something you'd be interested in working together on?
- Would you like to explore what it would look like to work together more closely on that?
- Is this something you'd like for us to tackle together?

Step 8: Share Your Offer

At this point, your prospect has said yes, they want to know how they can work with you to achieve their goal. Congrats! That means it's time to share your offer with them and bring them on as a client!

When it comes to this part of the sales conversation—also known as the "close"—there are a million different ways to structure it. I'm going to offer one example here, but the more you experiment with what feels best for you, the better your close rate will be.

For now, it's important to master the three most basic elements of the close:

1. Present your offer
2. Get feedback from your prospect
3. Talk about the logistics and investment

Present Your Offer

When presenting your offer, or pitch, it's best to lead with the two most important aspects of your program: the result it helps your clients achieve and the process by which you help them achieve that. In creating your offer, you got clear on both of those things, which means that you've already done most of the hard work. It's simply a matter of looking back to how you've previously defined your offer and fine-tuning the language to fit this context.

The formula for presenting your offer is, "My specialty is helping my clients achieve *x (goal)*, and the way we do that is pretty simple. First, we do *a (first step of your process)*. Then, we do...." And so on.

Here's a quick example:

> *My expertise is helping high-impact coaches create a consistent flow of leads, so they can spend less time worrying about marketing and more time enjoying working with clients.*
>
> *It's a pretty simple process. First, we get crystal clear on your ideal client, offer, and messaging so that we can pinpoint exactly who we're targeting and speak directly to their desires. Then, we help you implement a simple*

social media lead generation strategy designed to get you consistently booking calls with prospective clients. Finally, once that's happening, we guide you through the process of outsourcing pieces of your lead generation, so you can open up your capacity even more—whether that's to work with more clients or just work less.

As you can see with that example, it leads with the information most relevant to the prospect—what it's going to do for them and how it's going to do it. You also probably noticed that there are some notable components missing from the pitch, more specifically the program length, number of coaching sessions, and investment—all the nitty-gritty logistics. That's because logistics are, well, logistics. They don't excite people in the way that you need to excite your prospect. But don't worry, there will be a place for the logistics later on in this step.

It's also important to note that even though you've already done the work to clarify your offer, your pitch must directly reflect the pain points that your prospect has shared with you throughout your call. Too often, I see coaches who are struggling to close sales because when it comes to sharing their offer, the offer they pitch does not directly align with the pain points that their prospect has shared. It's like saying, "So you've told me that you really want to solve *abc* issues, so here's my offer that solves *xyz* issues" —presenting an offer that does not speak to the pain points the prospect has communicated.

While this doesn't mean that you need to pitch an entirely different offer to each prospect, it does mean that when you share your offer, it's important to highlight how each step addresses one or more of the prospect's pain points. If you're a fitness coach and your prospect is really interested in upping their cardio game, you're probably not going to emphasize the part of your program where you help your clients establish a strength training program. You'll probably still include that as part of your process when working with every client, but it doesn't make sense to highlight that as part of your pitch.

Get Feedback from Your Prospect

After presenting your offer, it's important to pause for a moment to do two things: Get some sort of feedback from your prospect and answer any questions they might have at this point.

The best way to do this is to ask a simple question, something like "Does that sound like it would help you achieve x (result)?" The purpose of this question is to focus on making sure—before even mentioning the investment—that this offer is a perfect fit. If it doesn't feel like a perfect fit to them, it's simply a matter of asking which parts of it are the most and least exciting so that you can begin to identify how you can make it a perfect fit for them.

If you've accurately summed up their pain points and have incorporated them into your pitch, though, your prospect will most likely say, "Yes—this is exactly what I need."

Talk About Logistics and Investment

Once you've gotten that "Yes—this is precisely what I need," it's time to move into talking about the logistics required to get your prospect enrolled—specifically, the investment.

Here's what this part of the close looks like:

> **Coach:** *Great! My program is 12 weeks long and the total investment, including everything we've talked about today, is $2,500.*

After sharing your program's total investment, *shut up*. Wait for your prospect to respond. This may feel a bit unnatural at first, but it's important to give them time to absorb what might be a bit of sticker shock.

If after a few moments, your prospect says that they're ready to get started, great! You've just made a sale. More commonly, though, they will say that it's bit more than they expected or that it's a little out of their price range or budget. In that case, it's wise to share any payment plans that you might have available:

> **Coach:** *It's certainly an investment. I do have a payment plan option; is that something you'd like to hear more about?*

> **Prospect:** *Absolutely.*

> **Coach:** *Like I said, the total investment is $2,500 for this 12-week program, so what I can do is offer a payment plan of either three months at $833/month or four months at $625/month. Does that make it more doable for you?*

This is the point at which one of three scenarios occur. Either they're ready to get started, want some time to think about it, or it's a hard no. If they're ready to get started, it's always best to take the first payment over the phone via credit card and to communicate what the next steps are for onboarding them as a new client.

If they want some time to think about it, *go ahead and book a follow-up call while you're on the phone.* Get a date on the calendar for no more than a week later, and frame it as an opportunity to check in, see where they're at, and see how you can support them.

If it's a hard no, let them know that you truly understand and ask if you can circle back around in a couple of months to see how they're doing. If they decline, respect that. But if they say yes, it might mean that they're not a hard no after all—that they're just a hard no at the moment.

ADDRESSING CLIENT OBJECTIONS

While there is a predefined flow for the strategy session, you need to understand that what I've presented here is the "ideal" strategy session. The reality is that not all sales calls will go that smoothly. The most common area where turbulence arises is around objections, which are the concerns that your prospects raise as potential reasons not to move forward working with you.

The most important lesson is that you don't have to be a jerk to get sales. *And you don't have to be a jerk when handling your prospects' objections. In fact, it can blow up in your face.* Remember Chris, the asshole sales guy who tried to make me feel like shit to get my credit card number? Before he tried to play his mind games with me, I was strongly considering buying the program. Being pushy lost him a $10k sale.

In this chapter, we're going to talk about the different types of objections and how to handle them with integrity—in a way that's aligned with your values and treats the prospect with dignity. But it's important to first understand objections on a deeper level. Objections, in their simplest sense, are excuses—whether valid or invalid, rational or irrational—that your prospect identifies as reasons not to work with you.

It may be jolting when you're on a sales call with a prospect who's been saying that your program is precisely what they need—until it's time for them to make a commitment. Suddenly, they seem to become an entirely different person, coming up with all the reasons they can't do it. That's because up until this point, you've been talking about change in a somewhat abstract sense; your prospect hears what you're saying, and it excites them. But when it comes time to take concrete action, the survivalist, animalistic part of their brain kicks in and says, "Hey, wait. We're safe right where we are. We know this is safe." That's because change sounds good...in theory.

Our subconscious brains—the survival part of our brains—views change as an unknown quantity, and anything unknown is not safe. Therefore, its prime concern is keeping things the same.

Your prospect's survival instinct is trying to keep them where they are, because even if their current situation is far from ideal, *it's familiar.* There may be lions and tigers and bears, but these are familiar challenges that they have adapted to surviving, even if it keeps them from being happy. When faced with the opportunity to do something differently, their brain tells them that maybe it's not so bad after all, that maybe they should just stay where they are.

This phenomenon doesn't mean that your prospect is lazy or a cheapskate, and it doesn't mean that they're not willing or ready to do the work to reach their goals—it simply means that they're human.

The problem is that this part of our brain often prevents growth beyond safety. Any type of growth, whether it's in our lives or business, involves some level of risk. When the opportunity for growth is on the table, our brain's default setting is to say, "Nope, no thanks. I'm good. I'm perfectly safe where I am."

As a coach, *it's your responsibility* to stand up for your clients' transformation. This means that sometimes you do have to coach them through limiting beliefs to help them make an empowered decision. Any sales coach will tell you that, but what really matters is *how* you approach this process.

Having worked with countless sales coaches in the past, here's some of the language that many of them teach their clients to use to close sales:

- "You're saying that you want *x* transformation, but if you were really committed, you wouldn't have a problem investing." (Sound familiar?)
- "How can you afford to move forward without it?"
- "Is fixing *x* problem not worth it to you?"

While it's true that you can't be a pushover who walks away from a prospect as soon as they object, don't buy into the false narrative that you have to be overly pushy—bordering on rude—to close new clients.

There's absolutely a middle ground here, something that lies between being an asshole and a pushover. You can challenge prospective clients' limiting beliefs and mental roadblocks without being an asshole, without emotionally manipulating them, and without making them feel attacked.

Ultimately, it comes down to emotional intelligence. In sales (and coaching, for that matter), it's critical to pay attention to and respond to the subconscious cues that people are giving you.

For example, if Chris had a modicum of emotional intelligence, he would have gotten the sale. But here's where he went wrong:

- When he started to challenge me directly and question my commitment, I retreated and shut down, essentially losing interest in working with his company. He didn't notice this.
- Even though my interest was waning, he said he required a refundable $1,000 deposit to book a follow-up call with him.
- Even though I had shut down and reverted to giving one-word replies, he accused me of being scared to move forward.

The tactics Chris used aren't inherently unethical, problematic, or indicative that he is an asshole (although the accusing me of being scared might be) because the truth is that some people *do* need to be challenged in a more overt and aggressive way. Some people respond well to that.

Most don't. I certainly don't, and most people I know don't either— which is why it's so important to pay attention and respond to the cues that your prospect is giving you. For example, if Chris was paying more attention to my responses, the conversation would have ended more like this:

> **Chris:** *Alright, I can take your credit card number whenever you're ready.*

Me: No, I'm not quite ready. I need to think about it.

Chris: I totally understand that, and I think you should think about it—it's a big decision that will impact your life forever. Let's set up a time to chat in a couple of days...what does your day look like on Wednesday? Are you free at 2?

Me: Yep, I can do that. Look forward to talking to you then!

If the call had gone that way, I probably would have ended up investing. Here's what makes this version of the conversation so much more effective:

- He affirmed my need to think about it rather than discrediting it. He didn't invalidate my thoughts and feelings.
- This more emotionally intelligent version of Chris respected me enough to respect my need to think about it before making a significant investment. He didn't try to weasel my credit card number out of me or dismiss my needs.
- He was assertive but not aggressive—assertive in the sense that he took the lead on scheduling a follow-up call, but not aggressive in that he didn't accuse me of being scared or uncommitted.

We're going to talk about handling more specific objections below, but there are four key points to handling any objections. Because at the end of the day, a script isn't going to do much for you—you will sell more and help more people by showing up authentically as yourself and by keeping these points in mind:

First, *listen, and make sure your prospect feels heard.* Listening is one thing, but it's an entirely different thing to make sure your prospect knows that they're being heard. This can look like mirroring back what they've said to you, but it also means articulating their problem more clearly than they could have themselves.

Second, *affirm your prospect's experience and recognize that it's real.* Whatever thoughts or emotions your prospect is experiencing are valid, if not necessarily rational. Affirm that those thoughts and emotions are valid and help them through the process of thinking rationally about them.

Third, *be assertive, but not aggressive.* Take a stand for your prospect's transformation, but don't be an asshole about it. If they're on a call with you, then they have some amount of trust in you—so live up to that trust by challenging them to become a better version of themselves.

Finally, *balance authority with intimacy.* People want to work with experts, yes, but they work with experts they know, like, and trust. It can be easy to focus on demonstrating your authority, but spend just as much energy building a close relationship with the prospect. Because ultimately, they'll decide based on how much they like and trust you.

HOW TO HANDLE OBJECTIONS

The best way to treat objections that arise is as valid concerns. Even if they don't seem valid or rational to you, they're still very real to your prospect. Therefore, when handling any objection, the best practice is to acknowledge and validate their concern, help them deconstruct the objection, and then to show them how your program benefits them directly in the context of their objection.

Acknowledging and validating your prospect's concern is as simple as saying something like, "I certainly hear that, and a lot of my clients deal with/have dealt with that before as well." The purpose of this is simply to emphasize that you're not glossing over their concerns and that you're genuinely listening to them.

Then, the best way to deconstruct your prospect's concern by asking them questions. It's best to start with, "Do you mind if I ask you a couple of questions about that?" and then to move into your questions about the objection. For example, if they're worried that they don't have enough time to commit to your program, simply ask them how much time they *do* have each week that they could commit. And then ask them where they might be able to reallocate time in their schedule to commit to the program. If they're spending hours every week watching Netflix, for instance, that might be an area where thy could reallocate time—if they're willing to do so.

Then, once you've deconstructed their objection, you finish the process of dealing with their objection by showing them how your program benefits them in the context of that specific concern. If their initial concern was that they don't have enough time to commit, once you've shown them that they *do* have enough time, transition into showing them how your program *saves* them time in the long run. If you're a fitness coach, you can tell them how much time they'll save by only doing the workouts that are going to make the most significant difference, or, on an even larger scale, that they'll have more time simply because they're going to live longer as a result of living a healthier lifestyle.

Most objections you encounter will fit into one of three different categories—money, time, or relationships. Either they're worried about the investment, time commitment, or their spouse/partner's approval. Fortunately, you can prepare for these objections by answering these questions to identify how your program benefits each of these.

Money Objections

- How will your program save them money?
- How will your program make them money?
- How much is it costing to do nothing?
- How will that cost increase over time?

Time Objections

- How will your program save them time or make them more productive?
- How will it help them get the result or transformation faster than working on their own or trying other methods/ solutions?

Relationship Objections

- How will your program ultimately benefit their significant other and/or the relationship?
- How will your program benefit their children or other family members?
- How will your program positively impact their social life?

CONDUCTING FOLLOW-UP CALLS

There are many coaches out there who claim that you can close every sale in an initial strategy session—that you can talk with a prospect for 45 minutes and close the sale right there and then. I've found that the people who are teaching that method are usually not using it themselves. Instead, on their own sales calls they take two, maybe three calls with a prospect before bringing them on as a client.

The answer isn't that you should or shouldn't close a sale in an initial 45-minute call, but rather to listen to your gut and move the process along naturally—instead of feeling forced to do a one, two, or three-call close. That means inevitably the need will arise for a follow-up call with a prospect—a second, or even third call wherein you close the sale.

The most common scenario for a follow-up call is when your prospect says they need to "think about it," which is a valid request on their part. When that happens on the initial call, it's best to go ahead and book a follow-up call while you have them there on the phone. One tactic for booking follow-up calls that works really well is to ask them how much time they'd like to think about it, and then to book the follow-up call for that day. For example, if it's Monday, and they say they need two days to think about it, suggest scheduling a call on Wednesday.

More important than when you book the follow-up call, though, is how you conduct it. In contrast to the strategy session, the follow-up call is much more fluid, and its purpose is to address any remaining objections that your prospect has and ideally to enroll them in your program.

The agenda for the follow-up call is fairly simple and straightforward:

1. Recap your prospect's pain points
2. Recap your offer
3. Ask if they'd like to get started

After beginning the call and exchanging pleasantries, do a quick recap of your prospect's three biggest pain points, and confirm that you didn't miss anything. Assuming they say yes, then quickly recap your offer, highlighting the three biggest steps in your process that align with your prospect's pain points. This should be fairly quick, and after summarizing your offer, check in again with your prospect to make sure they see how your offer directly solves their pain points, something like, "Does that sound like it would help you achieve x (goal)?"

Once you've gotten confirmation from your prospect, the next step is to transition the call to talking about next steps and bringing them on as a client. The best way to do this is to ask them if they have any remaining questions or concerns around how they can get started working with you. This is an opportunity for your prospect to share any remaining objections they may have, and, more importantly, for you to address them.

Once you've overcome your prospect's objections, and they have no remaining questions, the process is the same as the strategy session: Take their first payment over the phone and explain the next steps for getting them onboarded as a client.

IN CONCLUSION

IN CONCLUSION, the entire process of attracting your ideal clients is pretty simple. It's the process of finding your ideal clients, connecting with them, building relationships, having authentic sales conversations, and enrolling them into your program. And when you're clear on what you're offering, who you're serving, and how you communicate that, the process becomes even simpler.

In a nutshell, attracting new clients isn't as complicated as all the marketers out there want you to think it is.

The client attraction process you've learned in reading this book is one of the most effective out there today, primarily because it leverages social media tactics and techniques that evolve alongside the social platforms they're implemented on, and because it depends heavily on the most authentic and effective sales and marketing techniques that have stood the test of time: building genuine relationships with ideal clients. It's a strategy that, when you first learn it, *just makes sense*. And that's because it is indeed radically simple, especially compared to the complicated funnels and campaigns that seem to dominate the marketing space these days.

Although it is a simple process, it still requires work and effort to be effective. In and of itself, this book is not magic—it is not the one thing that will transform your business, nor is it the secret sauce that will make you rich in a matter of weeks. However, when coupled with consistent daily action, the strategies in this book will give you a steady flow of leads and clients. But it requires your action.

Assuming that you're reading this conclusion after reading the rest of the book in its entirety, you're probably itching to get started, excited to connect and have powerful conversations with your ideal clients. *That's called momentum*, and it's one of the most powerful tools in your arsenal. It will drive you to take those small actions every day, no matter what. And it's important to build that momentum every day.

There are a variety of strategies to build your momentum and stay motivated every day to implement your client attraction process, but there are two in particular that will make all the difference.

The first is *accountability*. Being an entrepreneur is a remarkable and freeing adventure, but one of the common difficulties is that you're accountable only to yourself. You're not accountable to a manager or boss—no one is checking up on you to make sure you're taking the necessary actions to make your business grow. For most folks, this means lower productivity and slower growth. When holding yourself accountable becomes a challenge, explore different external accountability structures that can keep you on track, like an accountability partner, reward system, or coaching. The important thing is to find an accountability structure that helps you maintain consistency and, even better, challenges you to reach higher.

The second is *support*. With this client attraction process, along with any other system or process in business, parts of it will come easier to you than others. You'll be excited to do some things, while other tasks will fill you with dread. You'll have questions about the best way to implement a specific task and need guidance along the way. *Find support.* There are many ways to get the support you need, whether that's coaching, an online course, a mentor, or mastermind. Entrepreneurship can be a lonely venture at times, but it doesn't mean that you have to be in it all alone. *Find the support you need.*

You likely picked up this book because you need more clients—because whatever you're doing in your business right now isn't working as well as you'd like it to be. Throughout this book, my responsibility has been to give you the tools you need to solve that problem, but now it's time for me to hand the responsibility off to you. Because from here on out, it's your responsibility to use those tools, and it's your responsibility to get your hands dirty to build the business you've envisioned for so long.

You've got this.

ACKNOWLEDGEMENTS

I hadn't originally planned to include an acknowledgements section, but the process of writing and bringing this book into the world has shown me just how many people have played a role in producing the book you're holding right now.

First and foremost, thanks go to the team who worked to make it reality, including Peg Robarchek, Tovi Martin, Brandon Love, Ashley Torres, and Heather Wylde Smith.

To my partner, Ruben, who has been with me every step of the way, and who has given me the support I need since day one. You're the love of my life, and I'm honored to be on this journey with you.

To my parents, Stephen & Melissa Ratliff, who first taught me what it means to love, what it means to grow, and what it means to strive for excellence. And to my brother, Benjamin, for cheering me on and believing in me.

To my grandfather, Jerry Hancock, for planting the entrepreneurial seed in me from a young age, and for tending it throughout my childhood. For serving as a trusted mentor, and for always having a funny story to tell.

To my entire family, named, and unnamed, for being part of my journey.

To the mentors and coaches who have made a bigger difference than you'll ever know, among them Mary O'Connor, Heather Wylde Smith, Hana Dhanji, Gareth Higgins, Brian Ammons, and Katherine & Danny Dreyer.

To the most understanding and loving group of friends a stressed-out entrepreneur could dream of, for being there for me through the highs and the lows.

Last, but certainly not least, to my clients, who have been a source of endless inspiration. Y'all are the real rockstars, not me.